# A TALE
## —— *of* ——
## TWO DOCTORS

# A TALE
## *of*
# TWO DOCTORS
*Unsung Heroes of Texas History*

GLORIA PEOPLES-ELAM

TATE PUBLISHING
AND ENTERPRISES, LLC

*A Tale of Two Doctors*
Copyright © 2016 by Gloria Peoples-Elam. All rights reserved.

No part of this publication may be reproduced, stored in a retrieval system or transmitted in any way by any means, electronic, mechanical, photocopy, recording or otherwise without the prior permission of the author except as provided by USA copyright law.

The opinions expressed by the author are not necessarily those of Tate Publishing, LLC.

Published by Tate Publishing & Enterprises, LLC
127 E. Trade Center Terrace | Mustang, Oklahoma 73064 USA
1.888.361.9473 | www.tatepublishing.com

Tate Publishing is committed to excellence in the publishing industry. The company reflects the philosophy established by the founders, based on Psalm 68:11,
*"The Lord gave the word and great was the company of those who published it."*

Book design copyright © 2016 by Tate Publishing, LLC. All rights reserved.
*Cover design by Bill Francis Peralta*
*Interior design by Jake Muelle*

Published in the United States of America

ISBN: 978-1-68352-660-5
1. History / General
2. History / United States / General
16.07.21

# Contents

Introduction . . . . . . . . . . . . . . . . . . . . . . . . . . . . . . . . . . . . . . . . 7

1  Robert Peebles and Austin's Colony . . . . . . . . . . . . . . . . . . 9

2  Richard Rogers Peebles and
   the Beginnings of a Nation . . . . . . . . . . . . . . . . . . . . . . . . 35

3  The Fight for Texas Independence . . . . . . . . . . . . . . . . . . 47

4  The Legacy of Stephen Fuller Austin . . . . . . . . . . . . . . . . 69

5  Stephen Fuller Austin: Father of Texas . . . . . . . . . . . . . . . 91

6  Dr. Robert Peebles's Life after
   San Felipe de Austin . . . . . . . . . . . . . . . . . . . . . . . . . . . . 103

7  Doctor Richard Rogers Peebles:
   Finding His Place in History . . . . . . . . . . . . . . . . . . . . . . 111

Epilogue . . . . . . . . . . . . . . . . . . . . . . . . . . . . . . . . . . . . . . . . 129

References . . . . . . . . . . . . . . . . . . . . . . . . . . . . . . . . . . . . . . 135

# Introduction

In researching for my book *An American Heritage Story*, I found two doctors by the surname of Peebles in Texas history. I wrote about them briefly in that book. These two doctors are often mistaken as being just one doctor. At least one genealogist, Anne Bradbury Peebles, did point this out in her *Peebles Ante 1600–1962*. Had it not been for extensive work by Ms. Peebles long before there was an Internet, there might never have been a distinction between the two.

In fact, many historians that I've encountered in my own research usually have thought that Dr. Richard Rogers Peebles was just mistaken to be Dr. Robert Peebles or vice versa. Even at the Dolphe Briscoe American History Center at the University of Austin, the librarian was astounded to learn of my own findings that there were indeed two doctors.

Both doctors came to Texas prior to Texas independence. One came from Ohio, and the other one from South Carolina and settled in Stephen F. Austin's Three Hundred colony. In writing this book, I wanted to give them their place in history. They both had a big part in Texas history and were a valuable part of the New Republic of Texas.

I began their stories from the time their ancestry came to America. The name Peebles was my ancestral name, which was changed by census takers to Peoples after the Civil War. Both doctors' ancestry began in Scotland. There isn't much significance in that fact other than their ancestry had not crossed paths in America, and, therefore, they had never heard of one another. The fact that they were both doctors seemed rather coincidental.

The chapters on Stephen F. Austin, the Father of Texas, I felt would add to the story significantly. Although Robert Peebles had been a personal friend of Austin, Richard Peebles was not.

He had, of course, known him and spoken to him, as did all colonists, but had not had time to develop a friendship. Robert Peebles's close association with Austin was an important reason to write about Austin and other Texas notables. Richard Peebles's association was with other notables of the colony as well.

As the reader will see in the story, the two men seemed destined to be where they were at that time in history. Now it is time to establish them in one book so that others can see some little known Texas history.

# 1

## Robert Peebles and Austin's Colony

> It is indeed desirable to be well descended,
> but the glory belongs to our ancestors.
>
> —Plutarch

The story of Robert Peebles began with his ancestral background in Scotland as far back as the first recorded Robert of Scotland in the 1300s. The Peebles name was associated with Scottish aristocracy through many generations, hence the name of Peebles, a shire in Scotland.

When the Great Rebellion began in Scotland with the Puritan Oliver Cromwell opposing the throne of King Charles I, many Scots fought as Royalists against Cromwell. Thousands of Scottish soldiers lost their lives in the conflict. Taken captive in 1649, Captain David Peebles, along with three hundred other captives, were to be executed. An escape was made for some, if not all, of those three hundred Royalists, many of them officers. Safe passage on ships sailing for the colonies was arranged. Captain Peebles was aboard the ship *Perfect* in 1649 as it sailed into Chesapeake Bay and up the James River to the Virginia Colony. His name is listed in the book *Early Virginia Families Along the James River, Volume II* as being a passenger on that ship. He had left his wife, Elspet, and his children in Scotland, hoping to send for them later. To have returned for them would have been certain capture and death.

Also recorded in that book is that Captain Peebles patented 833 acres along the James River in what was then Charles City County. Later, he and Charles Sparrow patented 2,500 acres on both sides of Birchen Swamp at the old Wyanoke Indian town.

He established the plantation *Bon Accord*, but before he could send for his family, word came that Elspet had died in 1652.

In 1655, he married Elizabeth Bisshop, the daughter of John Bisshop Sr., who was a Burgess member. David and Elizabeth had these children: Christine, Sarah, John, and Mary. John and Mary most likely died young as they aren't mentioned again in any text.

Captain Peebles only lived ten years in the new land. He was wounded in a battle with the Indians and died an invalid shortly thereafter. His daughters inherited a portion of the land, with his daughter Christine inheriting Bon Accord.

Christine married John Poythress, and the property was passed down through that family. The Poythress family had ties to John and Pocahontas Rolfe through the marriage of their son, Thomas Rolphe, to Jane Poythress. Christine Peebles Poythress was the sister-in-law to Thomas Rolphe, the son of Pocahontas, also known as Rebecca Rolfe.

Although not one of the original homes, this house is still referred to as Bon Accord and sits on the ancestral property previously owned by the Poythress family. A newspaper photo was obtained from the Prince George County Heritage Center of this home, which is no longer open to public viewing.

By the time Prince George County was created in 1703, Joshua Poythress, son of John and Christine, owned most of the nearby tract, Flowerdew Hundred, which had been granted in 1619. The Flowerdew Hundred property is still in existence today on the James River. In 1740, Poythress's daughter, Elisabeth, inherited Bon Accord. Her marriage to James Cocke opened the next chapter of the Aberdeen property.

Only one of Captain Peebles children is recorded to have come to the colonies to claim their inheritance. William Peebles I was only fourteen when his father came to the Virginia Colony. He had not seen his father in all that time, and he would meet his sisters when he came to claim his inheritance. He received a portion of that original tract but sold it later when he owned land in another county.

In 2012, on a trip to Virginia, I was able to see the very place where this history took place and take the pictures of one ancestral home still standing. Aberdeen is a working farm and vineyard and looks much the same as it did in the mid-1800s when it was built. Today Aberdeen is owned by a descendent of Capt. David Peebles. This plantation home is on the National Register of Historic Places.

In the mid-1700s, Dr. Robert Peebles's ancestor, Abraham, was in Camden, County, South Carolina. In 1776, the Revolutionary War was raging all around them. Some of the Peebles were listed as Quakers or Loyalist, but many of them fought against the British. In fact, one of the best accounts of the Revolution was written by Captain John Peebles Jr., a British soldier who documented the war. The Waxhaw or Buford Massacre, which took place during the Revolutionary War, was fought on land very near Abraham's property in Camden County. Fredrick Peebles was a young man who fought and died in that battle. Robert's grandfather, Lewis, was one who helped supply arms to the Patriots in the American Revolution.

Abraham Peebles's son Lewis had a son that he named David, most likely after Capt. David Peebles. It seemed that the Peebles family liked to name their children after those who went before them, having many Davids, Roberts, and Williams in the ancestral line. This David was born in 1769 in South Carolina. He became a doctor, taught the medical profession to others, including two of his sons, one of them being Robert, born in 1798.

Dr. David Peebles had given land and slaves to his children and most, if not all, did stay in South Carolina. However, Robert moved on from South Carolina. He went with his uncle John Peebles, first to Kentucky and then on to Louisiana, where he met and married Mary Trigg. Mary's family was a wealthy family in New Orleans, and Robert could easily have built his practice as a physician in that area.

If he had plans to go to Texas prior to New Orleans, he certainly heard about it soon enough. He may have met up with Stephen Austin at that time as he was frequently in New Orleans. What his wife might have thought about it probably didn't matter to the young doctor. He saw opportunity, and he was soon on the move again.

## Empresarios

During this era, there were about twenty-six empresarios who took out grants of land in Texas. Few of them succeeded in entirely filling their contracts, but their work was clearly shown by the growth and number of immigrants to Texas.

> The empresario system was favored by the Mexican government overall. The empresario made a petition to the Mexican government for permission to settle at his own expense a given number of families upon certain unoccupied lands. For each one-hundred families settled in Texas, the empresario was given five square leagues (22,142 acres) of land suitable for cultivation. If within six years from the date of the contract, the empresario had not settled the promised number of families, he lost many of his rights and privileges, while if he had not settled one hundred families his contract became null and void. (*A History of Texas Revised* by Anna J. H. Pennybacker, 1895)

## Texas and Coahuila

Until 1824, a separate province of Mexico, at that time Texas, Nuevo Leon, and Coahuila were one state. In that year, Leon and Coahuila became one state. Later, Nuevo Leon was made a separate state. Thus, the State of Coahuila and Texas had its capital located at Saltillo. This new arrangement caused the governor to live a great distance from Texas, making it necessary to appoint a chief of the Department of Texas headquartered in San Antonio. Although this officer performed many of the duties of governor, he was totally dependent upon his superior officer.

The Congress of the State of Coahuila and Texas adopted a Constitution, which was published in 1827. The state officers were not elected by the people, and this process was not popular with the Texans. The whole plan of union with Coahuila was unpopular with the Texans. The Texans were promised by the Mexican government that when a certain population was reached, there would be a separate state.

Every town of one thousand inhabitants was entitled to an *ayuntamiento* or common council, which was composed of the *alcaldes* or judges; the *sindico*, a recorder; and the *regidores* or aldermen. These were elected directly by the people. Those town officers often included those written about in this book and did much for the cause of liberty in the struggle for independence.

The *Texas State Historical Handbook* gives this description of the ayuntamiento:

> The ayuntamiento was the principal governing body of Spanish municipalities. It functioned as the town council and had a wide range of administrative duties. Its size varied and was generally based on the population of the town. The council members consisted of the alcade, who served as president, a varying number of regidors or councilmen, and a *síndico procurador*, the equivalent of a city attorney. Other

local administrators-police chiefs and fine collectors, for instance-sometimes held positions in the council, though often these additional members were not allowed to vote. The ayuntamiento was in most cases not a democratic institution. Often it received little voluntary support from the people it represented. Many offices were inherited, and others were sold by the crown or their current holders. Although elected officials did exist, by the late colonial period many ayuntamientos had to resort to forced service, for often few men of consequence volunteered to serve. The ayuntamiento managed police and security matters, hospitals, health measures such as the inspection of food markets and the removal of stagnant ponds, public roads, weights and measures, taxation, and agriculture. Though the powers of the ayuntamiento seemed wide, the body operated within the limits imposed by a higher authority, whether viceroy or governor. One of its primary functions, in fact, was to relay the orders of officials in Spain or Mexico to the local populace. In turn, the ayuntamiento often represented the interests of town citizens to the royal authority. Thus the ayuntamiento served as a mediating institution between local and central authorities.

Mexican independence did not fundamentally change local government. The number of ayuntamientos increased in Mexican Texas as the number of colonists grew. Spanish law had allowed any settlement of more than ten married men the right to a local council, and this right continued under Mexico. The constitution that unified Coahuila and Texas as a state merely formalized office-holding requirements by setting standards for age, residency, and literacy. By incorporating these minor changes, the ayuntamiento continued to function as a viable institution until the Texas Revolution.

## Stephen F. Austin's Three Hundred Colony

Moses Austin came from Missouri to San Antonio in 1820. He was aided by Baron de Bastrop as empresario to obtain permission from the Mexican government to settle three hundred families in Texas. Before he could accomplish the task, he became quite ill and died in June 1821. His dying request was that his son, Stephen, should take up the mantra and carry out the plans they had begun together.

Stephen Austin quickly took up his father's work with no urging. He was in New Orleans making arrangements for the colony when he learned that his father had secured a grant of land. He went directly to Natchitoches to meet the Mexican Commissioners, Seguin and Veramendi, who had been sent to meet the elder Austin. Being informed of the death of the elder Austin, the commissioners were quite willing to acknowledge Austin's claims. They were cordially received by the governor, who granted Austin permission to explore the country adjacent to the Colorado River and choose what lands he wished.

Austin selected for his colony the region lying south of the San Antonio road on the courses of the Brazos and Colorado Rivers. This included some of the most fertile land in that area and was the best choice he could have made. It was providence that seemed to be guiding his selection.

He returned to New Orleans and began advertising for colonists. To each man over twenty-one, he promised in the name of the Mexican government, six hundred and forty acres of land; if married, the man received three hundred and twenty more. Each child provided the father one hundred and sixty acres. The colonists were to pay Austin twelve and one-half cents per acre, as some general fund was needed to meet the expenses of surveying the land and obtaining titles. When a colonist built a mill or any structure of use to the public, he was given more land. Merchants were given town lots on which they might erect their stores or shops. Austin, as empresario on the fulfillment of his contract to settle those three hundred families, was to receive immense grants of land.

There was a huge stipulation that was required of all colonist. They had to become Roman Catholics, to swear to uphold the government of the Spanish king, and to furnish evidence of good moral character. With the promise of a better life and perhaps an immense fortune, the immigrants readily accepted the contract and were more than willing to follow Austin.

The "Old Three Hundred" were not just any three hundred families selected at random. Austin had been warned that he was solely responsible for the settlers, and they were selected with careful consideration. The settler's behavior would determine their success, especially in dealing with Mexico. Austin selected those he considered "better" classed for the most part, and as it turned out, only four of the original three hundred were illiterate.

While some of the people who came to Texas to settle were considered rude and ignorant, many were from the best families of both the North and the South. Perhaps they had left their old homes because of a failed business and thought the new West offered better opportunities. Some, surprisingly, came for their health while others were led by the sheer adventure of the whole process. Certainly it is true that the early Texans were men and women of more than ordinary courage and strength of character.

It was paying off to choose a smarter class of settlers to his colony. When it came to land, the new settlers knew to be smart. If they intended on being a farmer, they received "one labor" about 177 acres. If the settler opted to do a little more work, he chose to be a rancher. Thereby he received "one sitio," which was 4,428 acres. Most of the settlers, smartly, decided on being a rancher even though they had full intentions of only farming on the land. The farmers were located in three different groups surrounding the town of San Felipe de Austin, which was the nucleus of the colony.

The Old Three Hundred was not 300 in actuality. There were 297 titles issued for land, but not all the titles given for land were to families. Titles were also given to groups of two or three single men claiming to have partnership over the land. Only twenty-two of those types of partnerships were given to a total of fifty-nine men, which brought the total to 297 groups/families. There were 307 titles issued, but nine of the families received two titles each. Thus the title "the original old 297" didn't sound as good as "the Old Three Hundred."

The families were tasked with improving the land within two years and paying the state thirty dollars within six years, or they would forfeit their titles. Only seven groups/families failed to come up with the money for their lands.

Austin had his hands full with land grants and surveyors. Besides bringing the colonists to Texas, he strove to produce and maintain conditions conducive to their prosperous development. He faced issues of slavery, which was prohibited under Mexican law. The relationships between Anglo settlers, Indians, and Hispanic natives were always of grave concern. It was a continuous and rigorous battle for Austin, but one in which he felt it worth the fight.

> In recalling the hardships of Texas veterans, we must not forget that while one hand guided the plow the other was forced to wield the sword to protect the lives of wives and the little ones.
>
> —A. Pennybacker

## The First Colonists

Austin's plan was to establish two routes for entering Texas, one overland and one from New Orleans by water. He chose to come by way of the Red River, Natchitoches, and then the San Antonio Road. As he proceeded, he collected colonists at various points as he proceeded.

He sent by water tools and provisions, but as he didn't have the money for transport, he formed a partnership with Joseph Hawkins of New Orleans. A small schooner, *The Lively*, with about twenty men and generous supplies, sailed from New Orleans November 22, 1821. The schooner's captain had directions to wait for Austin at the mouth of the Colorado.

A misunderstanding, or in direct defiance, the boat stopped at the mouth of the Brazos. The voyage had been a grueling four weeks, and the men may have been confused. Tools, men, and provisions were unloaded at the mouth of the Brazos, and the schooner journeyed to the west.

After waiting for Austin for several days, the little group went exploring and finally settled a few miles up the river. They planted a crop, harvested it, and remarkably survived the elements for at least a year. Life was so hard that most of them returned to the United States.

*The Lively* came back to New Orleans, took on a new cargo and more passengers, and started once more for Texas. Near Galveston Island, the ship was wrecked in May or June 1822. The passengers, fortunately, were saved.

Austin, meanwhile, had reached Texas with quite a number of colonists. These settled on the Lower Brazos. Austin then hurried on hoping to meet *The Lively* at the appointed place. He anxiously awaited, but when no news came, he returned to the colony. Though greatly inconvenienced by the loss of the boat, he and the other colonists went on to begin the work of changing Texas from a wilderness to a land of homes, schools, and churches.

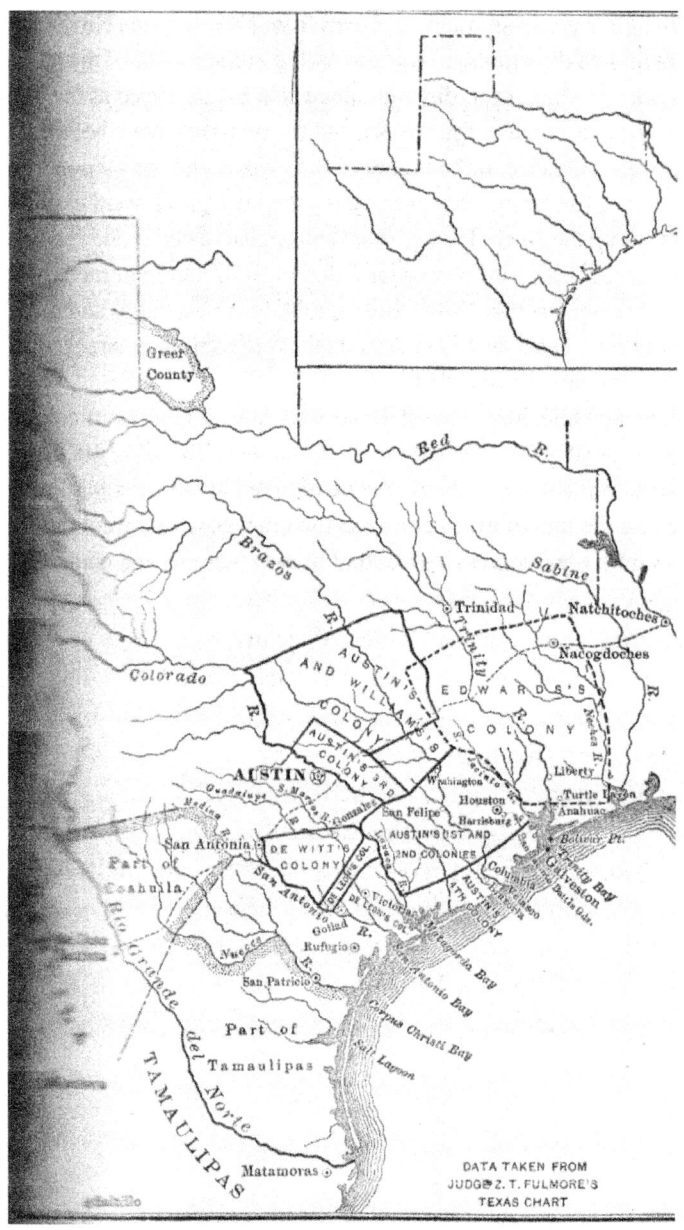

From a 1800s map showing the colonies and the routes

## Dealings with the Waco and Tonkawa Indians

During this era, the Indians were a source of danger to all the Texas colonists. Some empresarios had tried to win their friendship by kindness. Those efforts often failed, and then force was used.

An account from *A History of Texas Revised* tells a part of the story of the Native American Indians in that area, certainly not all of it, but in this account, the story is well worth writing about.

In July 1824, Austin's colony was so annoyed by thieves among the Indians that Austin sent a committee to make a treaty with the red men. He sent a Mr. Kuykendall, who wrote of this incident:

> They took with them some goods to barter with the Indians for horses. They crossed the Brazos at the San Antonio road and proceeded up the river on the east side to the Tawacanie village—thence they crossed over to the Waco village—the site of the present town of Waco. They were well received by the Indians, who had recently returned from their summer buffalo hunt and were feasting on buffalo meat, green corn and beans. They dwelt in the comfortable lodges, conical in shape, the frames of which were of cedar poles or slats and thatched with grass. The largest of these lodges (the council-house) was fifty-nine paces in circumference. The Wacoes and Tawacanies spoke the same language, and were essentially the same people. Judge D. thinks the two tribes could then number between two or three hundred warriors. They smoke the pipe of peace with the embassy and pledged themselves to peace and amity with the colonists. They had a great number of horses and mules. A small plug of tobacco was the price of a horse and a plug and half that of a mule.

The trickery of the Tonkawas became evident when Austin tried to induce them to cultivate the soil. He gave the chief,

Carita, hoes and other farming implements and an ample supply of seed corn. Carita promised that his people would clear the land in the Colorado bottom and plant the seeds. However, he had no intention of planting the seeds and growing corn. He made bread of the seed corn and, after it was all consumed, visited Austin with an absurd story. Carita said to Austin that the Great Spirit had told the Tonkawas not to raise corn but hunt, as they had always been accustomed to do, and look to their white friends for the staff of life. Austin informed him that he was inspired to say that Tonkewas would starve if they did not go to work. The Tonkewas never did till the soil.

Carita, a very shrewd Indian, indeed, and quite sharp at driving a hard bargain, said, "If Austin would trade with him he could cheat him out of his Colony." He may have thought so, but Austin was not about to let that happen.

## San Felipe de Austin

The town was founded in 1824 by Stephen F. Austin as the unofficial capitol of his so-named Three Hundred Colony. It became the first urban center in the Austin colony, which stretched northward from the Gulf of Mexico as far as the Old San Antonio Road and extended from the Lavaca River in the west to the San Jacinto River in the east. By October 1823, after briefly considering a location on the lower Colorado River, Austin, with the assistance of Baron de Bastrop, decided to establish his capitol on the Brazos near the settlement at which John McFarland operated a ferry. The site chosen was on a high, easily defensible bluff overlooking broad, fertile bottomlands. The location offered a number of advantages, including a central location and sources of fresh water from the Brazos.

The main area of Austin's Colony was located in Southeast Texas within an area bounded by the Lavaca and San Jacinto rivers, the San Antonio Road, and the coast. A small settlement called the "little colony" was also established along the Colorado River above the San Antonio Road, near the present-day city of Austin. The town of San Felipe, founded on the Brazos River in 1824, served as the capitol of the colony and the location of Austin's land office. Other towns founded during this period in Austin's colony include Matagorda, Brazoria, Columbia, Independence, and Washington-on-the-Brazos.

## Austin Goes to Mexico

The colony was established, and Austin thought it best to go to San Antonio and report to the proper officers of the progress. Meanwhile, a revolution was taking place in Mexico. It was necessary for him to go to Mexico to have his grant renewed. He also wished to have a full understanding concerning his rights in controlling the colonists. There was no time to be lost, and he made haste to go there. He left the settlement under the direction of Josiah Bell, who had recently arrived from Kentucky with his bride.

He arrived in Mexico in April 1822 finding the government in such disorder that he was forced to stay for a year. He was in a strange land, whose people already had a distrust of his country, and in the middle of the warring parties engaging in a revolution. His expertise and genius came through as he dealt with the Mexican government. He succeeded in renewing his grant and obtaining a statement of his power to lead the colony.

## A Deserted Colony

The year he was gone, the colonist began to think Austin had deserted them. Discouraged by his long absence, many of them drifted to the eastern part of Texas. New immigrants coming into Texas had stopped in East Texas instead of traveling on to the colony, which was not a wise move. They had no legal right to those lands and could be thrust out at any time.

Word quickly spread that Austin was back in the colony. Settlers began to return, and new life began again. New immigrants from various parts of world, and especially the United States, began to pour in.

In late 1823, surveyor Seth Ingram had undertaken the task of defining the boundaries of the five-league expanse of prairie and woodland encompassed by the municipality and platting the town. The governor of the Eastern Interior Provinces, Felipe de la Garza, proposed that the town's name should honor empresario Austin and the governor's own patron saint.

Don Luciano Garcia, the governor of Texas, was friendly to the colony and made efforts to help the colony succeed. In July 1823, he declared that San Felipe de Austin on the Brazos should be the capital. The town was officially founded in 1824.

A colony with so many odds against it was destined to take its place in history.

## The Year of Immigration

The year of 1825 was called the year of immigration. On March 24, the state Legislature of Texas and Coahuila passed a most liberal colonization law and declared "that the government was not only willing, but anxious to see Texas settled with intelligent, industrious, and liberty-loving citizens" (A. Pennybacker). Thus, many Americans not connected with the colony of empresario, led by the generous offers of land and the fair promises of the government, received grants of land directly from the state.

The town's layout was based on the Mexican town models of a regular grid of avenues and streets dominated by four large plazas. The settlement began to sprawl westward from the Brazos for more than a half mile along both sides of the Atascosito Road. By 1828, the community had grown quickly to about two hundred in population—three general stores, two taverns, a hotel, a blacksmith shop, and some forty or fifty log cabins provided goods, services and living quarters. Ten of the inhabitants were Mexican, and the rest were of American or European in origin. The males outnumbered the females ten to one. Usually referred to as San Felipe, it was the social economic and political center of the Austin Colony.

Several large cotton plantations were established in the bottomlands near the town during the 1820s, making San Felipe a busy trading center for cotton. As stock raising developed in the vicinity, small herds of cattle were driven from the town across the country to Nacogdoches in East Texas. There was a grist mill and lumber mill near the town, and the town was set to grow as the first "English school" was established by Thomas Pilgrim in 1829. Its enrollment was forty pupils, most of them boys, but by 1830, four schools were reported in the community with an enrollment of seventy-seven students. Literacy seemed to be a goal of early settlers. By 1835, the population approached six hundred, and many more settlers resided nearby within the boundaries of the municipality. It was by no means just a small burg. It was a growing and thriving town.

Stephen Austin built a residence on Bullinger's Creek, half a mile west of the Brazos. It was here he conducted his business as empresario of the government of his colony for four years. He handed over the responsibility for the management of most affairs to the ayuntamiento of San Felipe in 1828. The colonial land office was headquartered in the town, and Austin assumed an active role in its operation.

Regular mail service in the colony was inaugurated in 1826 when Samuel May Williams was appointed postmaster in San Felipe. There were seven postal routes that converged in San Felipe, and it remained the hub of the Texas postal service until the Revolution.

## Dr. Robert Peebles Arrives in the Colony

Dr. Peebles and his wife, Mary, came to Austin's colony on October 10, 1828. He was thirty years old, a strong and courageous young man. In less than a year, he secured a provisional license to practice medicine in the municipality of San Felipe de Austin. The *Texas State Historical Handbook* shows Dr. Peebles to have been on the Board of Physicians and on the first Board of Health in San Felipe in 1831. He became an associate of Dr. James Miller in 1834.

In the *Texas Handbook*, it is also documented that Dr. Peebles and Dr. Miller performed the first brain surgery in Texas. The patient obviously didn't survive as the surgery was done in an attempt to save his life if they could. The doctors literally "practiced" medicine in San Felipe and other places in those early times.

## Notable San Felipe Residents

Most of those early settlers arriving in the colony were said to be educated and with skills. As noted, Austin had intended for those who settled in his colony to have skills and to be useful in the building of towns. The many skilled craftsmen, doctors, lawyers, and other hard workers set about to build a town, and it grew rapidly.

The primary business of the colony was the introduction of new settlers and the distribution of land. As the contractor, Austin was the principal organizer and administrator of the colony. Besides Austin, several other people were involved in the colony's affairs. A land commissioner was appointed to represent the government and was responsible for administering and recording the land titles and organizing the archives of the colony. In July 1823, Governor Luciano Garcia appointed Felipe Enrique Neri, the Baron de Bastrop, as the first commissioner for Austin's Colony. Subsequent commissioners included Gaspar

Flores, Miguel Arciniega, Stephen F. Austin (acting as his own commissioner), and Robert Peebles.

Samuel May Williams had been hired by Austin in 1823 and performed a prodigious amount of work as secretary, title clerk, and agent for Austin. Williams was ultimately his partner in the final colony contract (more about Williams in another chapter).

By 1834, the duties of land office clerk were increasingly performed by Gail Borden Jr. Surveyors played an important role in the title process and included Rawson Alley, Gail Borden, Jr., John P. Borden, Thomas H. Borden, Samuel P. Browne, Horatio Chriesman, John Cook, Samuel Dickson, Jesse U. Evans, Isaac Hughes, Seth Ingram, John Jiams, Francis W. Johnson, James Kerr, George W. Patrick, John Goodloe, Warron Pierson, William Selkirk, Bartlett Sims, H. Smith, and Elias R. Wightman.

## Gail Borden Jr.

One of those men in the colony was an inventor, publisher, and surveyor. His parents, Gail and Philadelphia (Wheeler) Borden, could not have imagined their son, born in Norwich, New York, would make the name Borden a household name lasting into the twenty-first century as founder of a company that was early on a dairy. In 1816, the family moved to Indiana, where Borden obtained his only formal schooling, totaling not more than a year and a half. He would take that schooling and become a self-made man.

In 1822, he was in Mississippi in search of a milder climate to cure a persistent cough. While there, he became a surveyor and taught school. In 1826, he was an official surveyor for Amite County, as well as deputy federal surveyor.

In December 1829, Borden was at Galveston Island, where he raised stock in upper Fort Bend County and did some surveying. His brother, Thomas, had urged him to come to Austin's Colony to succeed him as surveyor at San Felipe. In 1823, Borden was named one of three members of the San Felipe committee of correspondence. He also assumed duties of colonial secretary for Austin in the absence of Samuel Williams. He formed a friendship with Dr. Peebles as they worked closely together in the day to day events of San Felipe.

One of the earliest newspapers in Texas, *The Texas Gazette*, began publication in San Felipe on September 25, 1829. The editor was Goodwin B. Cotton. Gail Borden was first a publisher. *Borden's Telegraph and Texas Register*, which became the unofficial journal of the revolution, was first published on October 10, 1835. The first issue, published in partnership with his brother Thomas and Joseph Baker, appeared in San Felipe, spreading the news so vital to the Texians. At this time, he also prepared the first topographical map of Texas and had resumed his responsibilities on the committee of correspondence.

Borden, as were so many others in that colony, establishing himself at a time that strong and well-educated men were needed. His name would be more related to milk than to his other accomplishments in early Texas. (More on his role in the Texas revolution in a later chapter.)

## The Land and Deeds

In addition to Dr. Peebles being appointed land commissioner by Austin, he was, for a short time, a sheriff. Although he had these important positions in the Three Hundred Colony, he is not always listed as having been in the colony on documents that list the original Three Hundred because he came later during the time of a larger immigration. Yet in letters sent to Austin by others and by Dr. Peebles, he was definitely there in the colony doing business. Some of that business had to do with lands and deeds and have been recorded in letters and in books.

It was a time of "land grabbing" in Texas, and many persons, because of time and distance, left legal procedures to be consummated later. In 1832, Robert Peebles and his partner at that time, Frank White Johnson, were accused of some illegal dealings in obtaining four hundred leagues.

In 1831, Dr. Peebles had obtained a headright of a league of land on the west bank of the Brazos River in what is now southeastern Fort Bend County. Experience in the trading of town lots in San Felipe kindled his interest in land speculation, which he pursued by taking up residence in the administrative center of Monclova, Coahuila. In 1835, he and his two partners, one of them Johnson and the other Samuel Williams, received the immense grant of four hundred leagues from the governor of Coahuila and Texas, to be parceled out as bounties for service in a new company of Texas militia. However, no such militia was organized, and the partners distributed the land in ten-league parcels among some two score Texas settlers. In 1835, Peebles returned to Texas, his Mexican dealings unknown and was made land commissioner for Austin's colony. He ignored the Consultation's decree of November 1835 to cease the issuance of land permits. Dr. Peebles still owned vast properties along the Brazos and other areas, having bought thousands of acres from the Mexican government.

At least one of the deeds was found at the Briscoe Center for American History at University of Texas at Austin. The deed has the signature of Robert Peebles and the signature of Thomas H. Borden. The other signature is a Mexican official, and the deed is written in Spanish. As mentioned, Thomas Borden was a surveyor and was the first of the Borden family to come to Texas to the Three Hundred Colony

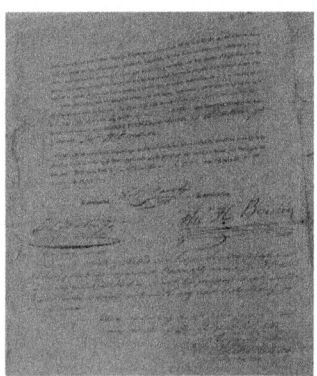

The Mexican deed of Robert Peebles,
courtesy of Briscoe Center for American History

Below: his partners in the land deals and two of the men who
held positions in the government at San Felipe de Austin
were Frank W. Johnson and Samuel May Williams.

Frank W. Johnson

Samuel May Williams

## A Note from a Noted Texas Hero

The original of the following note is also at the Dolphe Briscoe library. It was particularly exciting to find this note in the archives, especially because of the person who issued it:

> "I hold a title from (Mexican name) for three leagues of land which he sold in his life time to Dr. Robert Peebles _____ to which Peebles is entitled to a deed where in calls_____ June 18th 1834. Then the signature of William Barrett Travis."

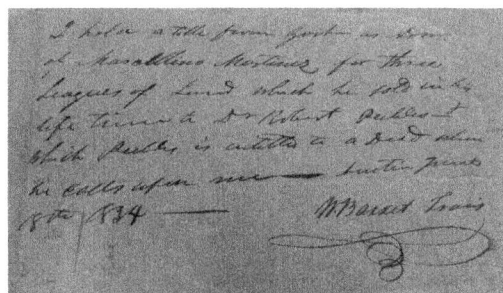

William Barrett Travis note courtesy of Briscoe Center for American History

## Beginnings of a Nation

The growth and progress made during the era was phenomenal. In 1820, there were not more than four thousand civilized inhabitants in Texas. By 1830, the state grew to about twenty thousand Americans alone. From the Sabine to the Neuces, empresarios had taken out grants until the province was covered. Towns like Columbia, Brazoria, Gonzales, Victoria, San Felipe de Austin became as familiar as Bexar, Goliad, and Nacogdoches.

Fertile farms, rich vegetation, blooming gardens where only waste places once stood were growing in vast numbers. These American colonists were not wild adventurers but home seekers. They came to raise families in this land of opportunity, to live and to die in the land.

Many foreigners came during that time to seek new opportunities. Ending this chapter with the account a young German girl describes the determination it took to overcome the hardships. It is also an account of life in Austin's colony.

Frederick Ernest, a German bookkeeper immigrated to America, upon hearing of the generous land grants offered by the Mexican government, decided to settle in Texas. His daughter, Caroline von Hinueber, tells the following story:

> When my father came to Texas I was a child of eleven or twelve years…We set sail for Texas in the schooner *Saltillo*.
> 
> The boat was jammed with passengers and their luggage that you could hardly find a place on the floor to lie down at night. I firmly believe that a strong wind would have drowned us all. We landed at Harrisburg, which consisted at that time of about five or six log houses, on the third of April, 1831. Captain Harris had a saw mill, and there was a store or two, I believe. Here we remained five weeks, while Fordtran (a friend) went ahead of us and selected a league of land…While on our way to our new home, we stayed at San Felipe for several days at Whiteside's Tavern. The courthouse was about a mile out

of town, and here R. M. Williamson, who was then the alcalde, had his office. I saw him several times while I was there, and remember how I wondered at his crutch and wooden leg. S. F. Austin was in Mexico at the time, and Sam Williams, his private secretary, gave my father a title to land which he had originally picked out for himself. My father had to kiss the Bible and promise, as soon as the priest should arrive, to become a Catholic…My father was the first German to come to Texas with his family. He wrote a letter to a friend in Oldenburg, which was published in the local newspaper. This brought a number of Germans, with their families, to Texas in 1834.

In the colony, Austin was, in most respects, the absolute ruler. Seldom does a man who has unlimited power govern with such mildness as Austin did. He never married. He had no time to even court a woman, devoting himself entirely to his people. He knew how to be severe when duty demanded. Several disorderly men were banished from the colony, and some were flogged. Yes, flogging was a form of punishment in those days.

The people in this Texas history tale all were a big part of Texas independence. Names like William Travis or Gail Borden Jr. will be recognized from history, but others like Dr. Robert Peebles will be looked over as having done little for the cause or for the Republic. He was a hero as much as any of the other men.

# 2

## Richard Rogers Peebles and the Beginnings of a Nation

> If the American Revolution had produced
> nothing but the Declaration of Independence
> it would have been worthwhile.
>
> —Samuel Eliot Morison (1887–1976)

William Peebles was born in 1745 in Scotland in the Shire of Peebles, twenty-five miles south of Edinburgh. He had been born into an aristocracy of many Peebles men who served in many capacities to the Crown. The background of this Peebles family is of a strong Scottish heritage, although their ancestors came by way of Ireland to the Colonies. As a young man, he left Ireland to come to the colonies, settling in Pennsylvania in Cumberland County.

He settled at Shippensburg, the oldest community of the Cumberland Valley, and the second oldest west of the Susquehanna River in Pennsylvania. July 1730, twelve Scotch-Irish families came to the Cumberland Valley and built log cabin homes along Burd's Run. Shippensburg began as the western outpost of colonial settlement. This was a big draw for other families coming to the Colonies from Ireland and Scotland.

At the onset of the Revolutionary War, William was thirty-one years old. He raised a company of soldiers for the war effort and fought valiantly against the British until he was wounded in the Battle of Flatbush on Long Island by the Hessians on August 28, 1776. He died of his wounds on September 5, 1776.

Grave of Captain William Peebles

He left his widow, Elizabeth "Betsy" Finley Peebles, to care for their three young children. The Finleys were prominent in Shippensburg, and with close-knit family and community, Elizabeth and her children were well taken care of.

Captain William McCracken had been a close friend of Captain Peebles and fought in the battle of Flatbush on August 2, 1776. After serving for a time as second lieutenant in Captain Matt Scott's company of State Regulars, he was commissioned as captain of the Thirteenth Regiment and transferred to the Pennsylvania line. Captain McCracken was assigned the sad duty of breaking the news of his friend's death to the widow. There was a story that he married Elizabeth within two days of delivering the sad news, but records show they married in 1778 in Cumberland County.

Elizabeth Finley was born in Cumberland County September 16, 1747. She was the daughter of John Finley, her family being some of the earliest settlers to that area. John's brother, Samuel, was the first president of Princeton College.

It was written in some accounts that Elizabeth was quite a woman and most determined in whatever she set her hand to do. She had married William Peebles in 1767. In 1778, she married William McCracken, and he died January 6, 1803. Lastly, she married William Rippey sometime after 1803, and he died in 1819. She was either drawn to those men named William, or it was a coincidence. She died September 16, 1832, in Big Springs, Cumberland County, at eighty-five years of age.

She had children by her second husband, and for them, there is a legacy, but for this tale, the concerns are the offspring of Captain Peebles. John, the son of Elizabeth and William Peebles, was born near Shippensburg on November 21, 1769. In 1795, he married Margaret Rodgers, born in Shippensburg, May 13, 1777. She was the daughter of Richard Rogers and Rachel Denny.

Five of their children were born in Shippensburg: William, namesake of his patriot hero grandfather, born November 16, 1796; Rachel Rodgers, born July 28, 1798; Elizabeth, born September 1, 1880; Fanny Denny, born July 3, 1806, but died at age 1; and Jane Finley, born February 23, 1806.

In 1807, John and Margaret, hearing of opportunities in Ohio, decided to leave their families in Pennsylvania and begin a long and rigorous journey. They most likely traveled on a wagon train with other families for safety against marauding Indians and bandits.

The still young United States of America was building an infrastructure of roads and canals for the expansion westward. The Braddock Road, or the Cumberland Road, had begun, but its extension, later known as the National Road (today Highway 40), was far from being finished. Although the National Road was the first road built with federal funds, it was mostly paid for as a toll road. Toll roads are not new, and the way west was in, some respects, made possible with toll roads. These were also developed from many of the well-traveled Indian paths.

However, to get to the Ohio River, which would take them to their destination of Portsmouth, Ohio, they would have to travel the western half of Pennsylvania by way of those rugged roads that would take weeks to maneuver just to get to the river. Upon reaching the river, they would sell the covered wagon and travel by flatboat to Portsmouth, Ohio, near the mouth of the Scioto River.

This must have been a difficult trip with four small children, one of them being Jane, just a baby. William, John, and Elizabeth, even though she was seven years old, would have been expected to work as they traveled along through those miles of wilderness in Pennsylvania and then by flatboat on the river. The hazards were monumental, and such a venture on the part of this pioneering family and all early pioneers is commendable.

The trek along rugged paths in Pennsylvania was hard enough, but the dangers posed by the river held even greater dangers. There were storms that could come up without warning, rapid waters that could cause a boat to capsize or break up on shore, and the ever-present dangers of Indians and bandits that would travel along the banks of a river. Traveling along with other flatboats did afford some safety, although at times flatboats collided. This mode of travel was so prevalent that often, a river was overloaded with them. It took at least a week and possibly two on the river to go to Portsmouth. By the time they reached their destination, they would most assuredly be ready to put their feet on dry land.

Example of a flatboat or keelboat

Flatboats, upon arrival at their destinations, were sold and dismantled. It was a time long before the steamboats that could travel up and down rivers. The river was a one-way trip. On arrival at a destination, or to travel back up river, was done by horseback or wagons. From Portsmouth, the Peebles family then loaded their belongings on a wagon and went to Chillicothe, Ohio, where they spent the next several years.

How they made a living in Chillicothe was not clear. At that time, Ohio was filling up with new settlers seeking a life in the new frontier. The opportunities for an industrious family were varied, and education for their children was available in a growing town on the new frontier.

While in Chillicothe, Richard Rodgers Peebles was born January 10, 1810. Margaret, was born November 10, 1811; John Geddes in November 30, 1813; and Joseph Scott in June 19, 1817. The family was growing, and this may have meant a need for a better job in a place that provided for better education as well.

In April of 1819, they once again moved, now with eight children. This time, they traveled down the Scioto River on a flatboat from Chillicothe to the Ohio River at Portsmouth. Here John became a banker in the fast-growing city on the river, where they raised their family with good educations. The Peebles family became a prominent and well-known family in Ohio and in Pennsylvania.

## The Geddes

This family is of Scotch-Irish descent and became important to the Peebles family in Pennsylvania. James Geddes, along with his wife and three sons—Paul, William, and Samuel—emigrated from County Antrim, Ireland, to Pennsylvania in 1752. William settled in Cumberland County and was the father of seven children. His second son, John, was born in 1766, studied medicine, and practiced at Newville, Cumberland County, until his death in 1740. He married Elizabeth Peebles, daughter of Captain William Peebles. John Peebles Geddes, the third child of James

Geddes, was born in 1799. He studied medicine and practiced with his father until his death in 1837.

The Ohio Peebles family remained close to their relatives still in Pennsylvania. The roads were constantly being improved, but travel from one eastern city to those in the west was still long and rigorous. It was a mode of travel that prevented families from seeing one another on a regular basis, perhaps only once a year at best. Letters were the best way to stay in touch.

Richard Rogers Peebles was inspired by his uncle Dr. John Peebles Geddes. In fact, Dr. Geddes paid for Richard to attend the medical college in Cincinnati. He received his degree and began to make plans for where he would set up practice.

It was 1835, and there was a rumbling in Texas with skirmishes already being fought with the Mexicans. Tensions were mounting in that Mexican territory, but young Dr. Richard Peebles decided to make his way to Texas. One has to wonder if his family opposed this dangerous move.

## Washington, Texas

The town of Washington was established in 1833 just north of San Felipe de Austin and on the Brazos River. It was called Washington at that time but became Washington-on-the-Brazos after the Civil War. It is in the upper northeastern corner of what is now Washington County.

In 1821, Andrew Robinson's family and other members of the Old Three Hundred settled near the future town site. By 1822, Robinson was operating a ferry at the La Bahia crossing of the Brazos. In 1824, he obtained a grant of half a league from the Mexican government. A settlement named La Bhia developed at the much traveled ferry crossing.

In 1831, Robinson gave one-quarter league to his daughter, Patsy, and son-in-law John W. Hall. Recognizing the site's commercial potential, Hall surveyed and laid out a town in

December 1833, when Methodist leader John W. Kenney built his first residence.

After Captain Hall bought the remainder of Robinson's grant, he established the Washington Town Company. In 1835, with Dr. Asa Hoxey, Thomas Gay, and the Miller and Somervell Company, they began to promote sales of town lots. Hoxey, a former resident of Washington, Wilkes County, Georgia, named the new town after his hometown.

By this time, Washington had become a supply point. Attracted by its location on the river, on or near major roads, merchants and tradesmen from neighboring communities settled in the new town. Washington's commercial growth resulted from provisioning emigrants to the interior and from the surrounding area's increasing agricultural development and population.

The town was elevated on bluffs above the river and had a plentiful water supply from nearby springs. The location was more healthful and less prone to flood than that of settlements near the river's edge.

By the time Dr. Richard Peebles arrived there in 1835, it was a bustling town with hotels and taverns for travelers. Lawyers, doctors, and surveyors offered their services. Tailors, dressmakers, and hairdressers and barbers kept people looking good. The local general mercantile store sold or traded for the goods necessary for daily living.

Ferry Street ran through the middle of the town and down to the river. It seems like a bit of overkill, as there were three doctors on that same street. There was one lawyer, one Baptist preacher, a tavern owner, and a sheriff. There must have been a need for three doctors with so much activity.

The townspeople of Washington greeted many visitors. Stagecoach lines came through town and connected Washington with other Texas towns. The Brazos River brought many travelers to small towns up and down the river. Some steamboats were beginning to make their way up and down the river, carrying goods and services to the area residents and businesses.

## Some Colonists Expected Much

In the ten years since that year of immigration in 1825, the settlements had grown in numbers. They were coming from many different counties, and about ten families from England had arrived in Texas.

One woman, with her son and daughter, stopped at Harrisburg. She was a dressmaker and a milliner. Seeing a small and crudely built town, she was very much disappointed as she had brought a stock of millinery goods from New York with expectation of finding a large city.

One man, Mr. Page, seemed to be the leader of the group. He had a wife and small baby and seemed to be a smart man, as the account read. The group was good people but seemed so sadly out of place in the small and rustic Texas towns. They had elegant clothing, silverware, and some fine furniture. Not one of them knew anything about farming or country life as they had been reared in the city of London, England, yet there they were, and they were going to make the best of it.

The lives of the new immigrants to the Texas towns and especially to Washington may never have expected such hardships. They were coming from well-established cities around the world. Although the United States was a relatively young nation, the communities and cities were well established, as many of the immigrants came to the colonies in the 1600s. Washington was just being built, and there were no comfortable amenities to be had.

[Map of Washington, Texas showing streets (Main Street, Market Street, Austin Street, Water Street, Ferry Street) and buildings including Independence Hall, Visitor Center, Noah Byors blacksmith, Thomas Heard doctor, John Lott tavern owner, Daniel Friar ranger, S.R. Roberts hotel owner, B.B. Goodrich doctor, Samuel Heath carpenter, Martin & Clow general mercantile, Joseph Chance lawyer Militia Captain, R.R. Peebles doctor, Z.N. Morrell Baptist preacher, John Lott & Jack Hall livery stables, David Ayers educator; Brazos River and Navasota River with Ferry Crossing.]

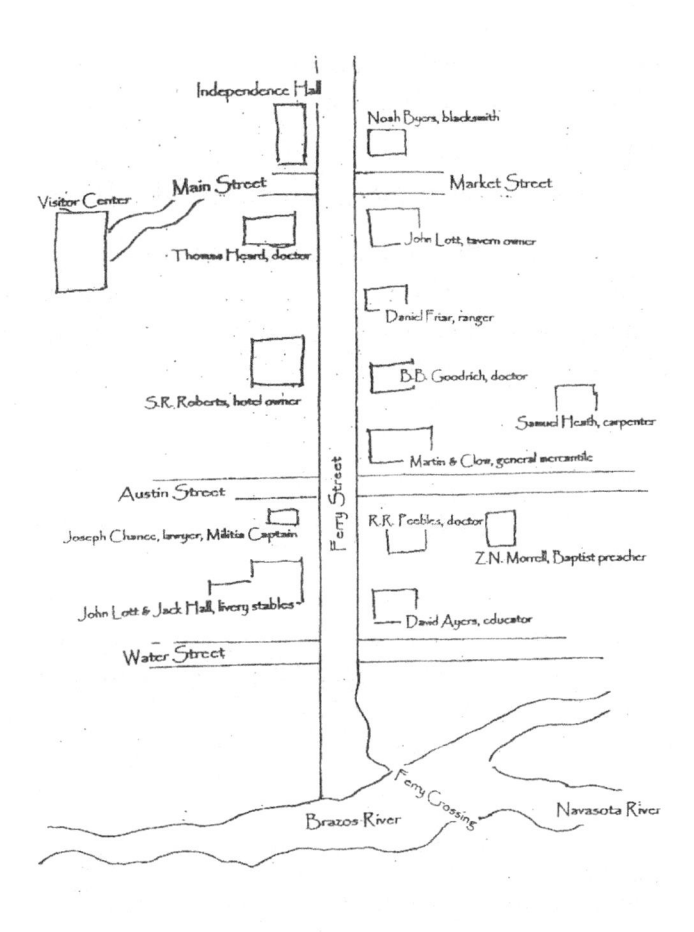

Washington, Texas

Map courtesy of Washington-on-the-Brazos State Park Visitor's Center

The map is a crude drawing showing the layout of Washington as it was at that time. Notice the location of Dr. Richard Peebles's office. Today, it is Washington-on-the-Brazos State park. None of the original buildings remain.

Even though everyday life for the inhabitants of Washington seemed quite normal, there was disturbing news in the newspapers. The talk around town, especially at the taverns among the menfolk, was getting intense. The town was about to become famous.

In December 1835, Washington became General Sam Houston's headquarters and the concentration point for Texas army volunteers and supplies. At that time, the residents numbered only one hundred, but with the army volunteers going in and out of the city, it became a hive of activity.

Dr. Richard Rogers Peebles, as a new young doctor, would be a part of a revolution to seek independence from Mexico. His letters home would have most likely been of grave concern to his family as he wrote of the goings on in Texas and especially in Washington.

# 3

# The Fight for Texas Independence

> I leave this rule for others when I'm dead.
> Be always sure you're right then go ahead.
>
> —David Crockett (1786–1836)

In 1830, the Mexican government issued a law that placed restrictions on the settlers and begin to stir the waters of revolution.

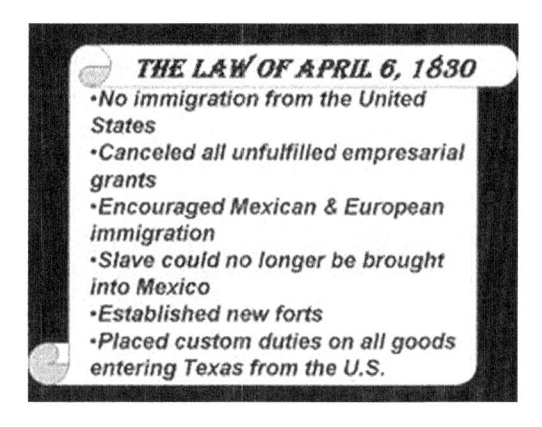

**THE LAW OF APRIL 6, 1830**
- No immigration from the United States
- Canceled all unfulfilled empresarial grants
- Encouraged Mexican & European immigration
- Slave could no longer be brought into Mexico
- Established new forts
- Placed custom duties on all goods entering Texas from the U.S.

In 1831, Mexican authorities had given the settlers of Gonzales a cannon to help protect them from frequent Comanche raids. Over the next four years, the political situation in Mexico deteriorated, and in 1835, several states revolted. As the unrest spread, Colonel Domingo de Ugartechea, the commander of all Mexican troops in Texas, felt it unwise to leave the residents of Gonzales a weapon and requested the return of the cannon.

When the initial request was refused, Ugartechea sent one hundred dragoons to retrieve the cannon. The soldiers neared Gonzales on September 29, but the colonists used a variety of excuses to keep them from the town while secretly sending messengers to request assistance from nearby communities. The Mexicans had come to Gonzales demanding the cannon from the colonists in order to disarm them. It was refused, and the Mexicans were driven back to San Antonio. It was expected, however, that they would return immediately with reinforcements, and Col. William Wharton was trying to collect a force strong enough to check them again. He sent the following proclamation:

### ARM, ARM AND OUT NOTICE

> I am just now leaving for the camp at Gonzales. All who are backward or refuse to go without the best excuse in the word will in the remorse and bitterness of soul, say to themselves, in after times, the gallant have fallen in vain! My countrymen and friends have won immortal renown—or have bled and fallen fighting my battles, and fighting for the great principle of human liberty, and I was not there. Let all who wish to avoid this heart-rending reflection march immediately to the camp at Gonzales. Every person who cannot go himself, and who withholds a horse or gun from those willing to go will be considered a traitor to his country and therefore infamous. Let no one, however, stop for want of a horse; soldiers who are in earnest have often marched on foot ten times as far as from here to San Antonio.

## William H. Wharton

Within two days, up to 140 Texians gathered in Gonzales, all determined not to give up the cannon. On October 1, settlers voted to initiate a fight. Mexican soldiers opened fire as Texians approached their camp in the early hours of October 2. The first skirmish between the Texians and the Mexicans occurred on October 2, 1835. After several hours of firing, the Mexican soldiers withdrew.

Although the skirmish had little military significance, it marked a clear break between the colonists and the Mexican government and is considered to have been the start of the Texas Revolution. News of the skirmish spread throughout the United States, where it was often referred to as the "Lexington of Texas."

The battle flag of the fight at Gonzales

This battle flag of Gonzales means a lot to Texans today. In his inauguration speech at the Texas Capitol, Governor Greg Abbot referred to this flag and that Texans would, if need be, stand up once again to a tyrannical government.

Just prior to the revolution, San Felipe ranked second in Texas only to San Antonio as a commercial center. Its close proximity to the Brazos River made it easy to transport goods on keelboats between the town and various coastal ports. Steamboats in the 1830s had gradually begun to appear on the Brazos, but most articles of commerce were still carried overland to the coast by wagon. In 1835, the population approached six hundred, and many more settlers resided nearby within the boundaries of the municipality. In view of its significance, it was inevitable that San Felipe should play an important role in the events of the Texas Revolution. The conventions of 1832 and 1833 were held in the town, and as the site of the Consultation of November 3, 1835, San Felipe served as the capitol of the provisional government until the Convention of 1836.

On October 15, 1835, each municipality in Texas was to send delegates "selected for their wisdom, honesty and their deep interest in the welfare of their country" to what was called a Consultation at San Felipe de Austin. It was so named a Consultation in order not to offend the Mexican Government, which believed a Convention was a revolutionary body. On November 3, 1835, Branch T. Archer, president of the Consultation, opened the sessions with an address in which he declared that Texas was not "battling alone for her rights and liberties." In a way, he was saying that Texas was not ready to declare independence. There was hot debate as to whether the Consultation should declare for the Independence of Texas.

By the end of the year in 1835, there was not a Mexican in arms against the Texians north of the Rio Grande, but beyond that river, an army was being formed to subjugate the Anglo-Americans or drive them beyond the Sabine. Preparations began in August 1835 when the Mexican government learned of what it considered the "perfidy, ingratitude and the restless spirit" of the colonists. In December, President Santa Anna placed the Mexican government in the hands of others and assumed personal command of the army. Recruits had been assembled from all parts of the republic, and the president was surrounded by the most distinguished commanders of which Mexico could boast. The troops, so ran an official proclamation, were "to sustain the honor of the country" and "cover themselves with glory." The intention was to crush the rebellion of the Texians.

Public sentiment, then as now, moved slowly, but on November 15, a meeting at Nacogdoches favored an unequivocal declaration of independence. One month later, the citizens of Brazoria took similar action, and by Christmas Day 1835, the volunteers at Goliad and the people of San Augustine and Columbia had requested the forthcoming Convention to declare for independence. Governor Henry Smith of Columbia had all along favored this action, and in January 1836, when Stephen F. Austin and Sam Houston joined with William Wharton and Branch T.

Archer in urging this course, there was hardly a man of prominence in Texas who opposed it.

By the end of January 1836, the Mexican expeditionary forces numbering more than six thousand disposed to various locations. On February 12, the main body of the army reached the Rio Grande. Eleven days later, a vanguard was encamped on the heights of Alazan, overlooking San Antonio.

## David Crockett Comes to Texas

In January, 1836, David Crockett, former United States Congressman, had just left Tennessee. He came to Texas for the purpose of assisting the struggling patriots. He had not been reelected to Congress, and he wrote this to the people: "You can all go to hell! I am going to Texas." The *Niles Weekly Register* in Baltimore, Maryland, April 9, 1836, upon hearing of the fall of the Alamo had this:

> A gentleman from Nacogdoches, in Texas, informs us, that, whilst there, he dined in public with col. Crockett, who had just arrived from Tennessee. The old bear-hunter, on being toasted, made a speech to the Texians, replete with his usual dry humor. He began nearly in this style: 'I am told, gentlemen, that, when a stranger, like myself, arrives among you, the first inquiry is—what brought you here? To satisfy your curiosity at once to myself, I will tell you all about it. I was, for some years, a member of congress. In my last canvass, I told the people of my district, that, if they saw fit to re-elect me, I would serve them as faithfully as I had done; but, if not, *they might go to h__, and I would go to Texas.* I was beaten, gentlemen, and here I am.' The roar of applause was like a thunder-burst.

While on his way to the Alamo, he stopped at the Swisher resident at Gay Hill to rest. John M. Swisher was a young boy and recounted this stay at his father's house.

> "His rifle I well remember. It was ornamented with a silver plate set into the stock, upon which was engraved, 'David Crockett.' He called it 'Bessie.'"

Young Swisher described Crockett in his account as being around six feet in height and about two hundred pounds. He thought him to be about forty years old, but he was at that time nearly fifty years old. He recalled that he was fond of talking and had an ease and grace about him that rendered him irresistible.

> "During his stay at my father's house it was a rare occurrence for any of us to get to bed before twelve or one o'clock. He told us a great many anecdotes. Many of them were commonplace and amounted to nothing in themselves, but his inimitable way of telling them would convulse one with laughter.
>
> I shall never forget the day he left us for San Antonio. We watched him as he rode away by the side of his young traveling companion (B.A.M. Smith) with feelings of admiration and regret. We little thought how soon he was to perish—a martyr to the cause of liberty.

Congressman David Crockett

## A Plea from the Alamo

Colonel William B. Travis was ordered by Sam Houston to raise one hundred men to reinforce the garrison at San Antonio. He had reported in January that after two weeks of strenuous effort, he had only been able to enlist thirty men. Of course, Crockett was one of them. Nonetheless, the siege began just as Colonel Travis sent out a letter for help. That letter is as follows:

>Commandancy of the Alamo Bejar,
>Feb'y 24th, 1836

>To the People of Texas and all Americans in the World.
>Fellow Citizens and Compatriots—I am besieged, by a thousand or more of the Mexicans under Santa Anna. I have sustained a continual Bombardment and cannonade for 24 hours and have not lost a man. The enemy has demanded a surrender at discretion, otherwise, the garrison are to be put to the sword, if the fort is taken. I have answered the demand with a cannon shot, and our flag still waves proudly from the walls. I shall never surrender or retreat. Then, I call on you in the name of Liberty, of patriotism and everything dear to the American character, to come to our aid with all dispatch. The enemy is receiving reinforcements daily and will no doubt increase to three or four thousand in four or five days. If this call is neglected, I am determined to sustain myself as long as possible and die like a soldier who never forgets what is due to his own honor and that of his country. VICTORY OR DEATH.

>William Barrett Travis, Lt. Col. Comdt

>P.S. The Lord is on our side. When the enemy appeared in sight we had not three bushels of corn. We have since found in deserted houses 80 to 90 bushels and got into the walls 20 or 30 head of Beeves.

William Barrett Travis

## Washington, Texas, and the Declaration

The letter was to no avail as not enough recruits came to their aid. During the siege of the Alamo, another assemblage was taking place. Delegates had been selected to meet at Washington again and this time to write the Texas Declaration of Independence. The Convention met on March 1, 1836, in near freezing weather in an unfinished building owned by Noah Byers and his partner, Peter Mercer. The building was rented by a group of Washington businessmen, one of them being Dr. Richard R. Peebles. It was the only structure large enough for the number of delegates, but just barely.

Washington was as one person remembered, "A rare place to hold a national convention. It is laid out in the woods; about a dozen wretched cabins and shanties constitute the city; not one decent house in it, and only one well-defined street, which consists of an opening cut out of the woods, the stumps still standing."

Although the town had an inn, most delegates could not find lodging. Certainly the town was not adequate for such a gathering, and one has to wonder why it was chosen. Perhaps because it was a place least expected to have a convention—out of the San Felipe capital and with an access to the Brazos. Even the building, still not finished, wasn't a place to comfortably house all the delegates.

Drawing of Independence Hall as it may have looked

Independence Hall in ruins at the turn of the century

Independence Hall reconstructed at
Washington on the Brazos State Park

## Texas Declaration of Independence Is Signed

One has to wonder if the young Dr. Richard Peebles was giving a second thought to his coming to Texas. It wasn't looking hopeful at this point, but perhaps he thought of it as the adventure of a lifetime, and perhaps it was just that. For sure, it was a time in history not to be missed, and he was in the big middle of it.

On March 2, 1836, the Declaration of Independence was signed.

The delegates at Independence Hall

Writer of the Declaration—
George C. Childress

Sixty men signed the Texas Declaration of Independence. Ten of them had lived in Texas for more than six years while one-quarter of them had been in the province for less than a year. Fifty-nine of these men were delegates to the Convention, and one was the Convention Secretary, Herbert S. Kimble, who was not a delegate.

- Jesse B. Badgett
- George Washington Barnett
- Thomas Barnett
- Stephen W. Blount
- John W. Bower
- Asa Brigham
- Andrew Briscoe
- John Wheeler Bunton
- John S. D. Byrom
- Mathew Caldwell
- Samuel Price Carson
- George C. Childress, writer
- William Clark, Jr.
- Robert M. Coleman
- James Collinsworth
- Edward Conrad
- William Carroll Crawford
- Lorenzo de Zavala
- Richard Ellis, President of the Convention and Delegate from Red River

- Stephen H. Everett
- John Fisher
- Samuel Rhoads Fisher
- Robert Thomas 'James' Gaines
- Thomas J. Gazley
- Benjamin Briggs Goodrich
- Jesse Grimes
- Robert Hamilton
- Bailey Hardeman
- Augustine B. Hardin
- Sam Houston
- Herbert Simms Kimble, Secretary
- William D. Lacy
- Albert Hamilton Latimer
- Edwin O. Legrand
- Collin McKinney
- Samuel A. Maverick Michel B. Menard
- William Menefee
- John W. Moore
- William Motley
- José Antonio Navarro
- Martin Parmer
- Sydney O. Pennington
- Robert Potter
- James Power
- John S. Roberts
- Sterling C. Robertson
- José Francisco Ruiz
- Thomas Jefferson Rusk
- William. B. Scates
- George W. Smyth
- Elijah Stapp
- Charles B. Stewart
- James G. Swisher
- Charles S. Taylor
- David Thomas
- John Turner
- Edwin Waller
- Claiborne West
- James B. Woods

The Texas Declaration of Independence was produced, literally, overnight. Its urgency was paramount because while it was being prepared, the Alamo in San Antonio was under siege by Santa Anna's army of Mexico.

Immediately upon the assemblage of the Convention of 1836 on March 1, a committee of five of its delegates was appointed to draft the document. The committee, consisting of George C. Childress, Edward Conrad, James Gaines, Bailey Hardeman, and Collin McKinney, prepared the declaration in record time. It was briefly reviewed, then adopted by the delegates of the convention the following day, March 2. On March 3, the members began signing the document. The Convention then proceeded to the writing of the constitution and election of ad interim government officials.

Like the American Declaration of Independence, which Thomas Jefferson wrote, the Texas Declaration of Independence begins with a philosophical statement of the nature of government, then enumerates the injustices suffered by the colonists and closes with a solemn declaration that the political connection between Texas and Mexico has forever ended. The document parallels somewhat that of the United States, signed almost sixty years earlier. It contains statements on the function and responsibility of government, followed by a list of grievances. Finally, it concludes by declaring Texas a free and independent republic.

Gail Borden had represented his town of San Felipe as one those fifty-five delegates. He had, in fact, printed the original Texas Declaration of Independence on his printing press, for which he was never paid. He had kept printing daily updates of the fighting until the Mexican Army overran his business, took his printing press, and threw it into a river.

## The Fight for Texas Independence Begins

On the sixth day of the Convention, Colonel Travis's appeal for assistance was read to the Convention. Robert Potter moved that the delegates adjourn and hasten to San Antonio. General Sam Houston declared that such an action would not only be folly but treason. Houston felt that the situation in the Alamo had been caused largely by the lack of governmental organization. He said it was the patriotic duty of the delegates to remain at their posts and provide Texas with a stable government. He was right. Although it seemed that the defenders of the Alamo needed every able-bodied man, it still would not have saved the Alamo or Texas.

A question often arises about those heroic and bigger-than-life individuals, who not only have built nations and empires but have saved countless lives. When men or women have a vision and/or are compelled to do something extraordinarily great that seems impossible to accomplish, from whence comes this motivation? Does it come from Almighty God? Did their own destiny place them at the exact moment in time?

There is no way of knowing, but every man at the Convention seemed to have the conviction that what they were doing was in all certainty going to bring a victory. Colonel Travis didn't doubt that he was there to accomplish a great purpose and have victory, and he was willing to die for the cause he believed in. Every cause needs a leader, and that man was Sam Houston. He knew that a government must be formed.

Stephen Austin was not at the Convention. He had gone to the United States, along with William H. Wharton and Branch T. Archer to seek help for the cause. That help was not to be forthcoming, and he would return with no promises. He was also becoming quite ill.

Dr. Robert Peebles was also at Washington, as was many men who were not actually delegates or signers of the Declaration. This may have been the first time the two Dr. Peebles actually met. Hopefully, the doctors had some time to converse, if not about their ancestry, then about the medical profession.

## The Runaway Scrape

After the fall of the Alamo, General Sam Houston's army retreated through San Felipe. On March 30, the small garrison under Moseley Baker remaining at San Felipe to defend the

Brazos crossing ordered the town evacuated and then burned it to the ground to keep if from falling into the hands of the advancing Mexican Army. The terrified residents hastily gathered what few belongings they could carry before fleeing eastward during the incident known as the Runaway Scrape.

Dr. Robert Peebles had already made haste to San Felipe. He loaded all the documents, deeds, and valuable papers onto a wagon. He took what he could of his own possessions and with his wife, Mary, headed for New Orleans.

Dr. Richard Peebles had wanted to ride with General Sam Houston to battle but was ordered to stay in Washington to care for the sick and wounded. However, he soon enrolled in Captain Joseph B. Chance's company and is listed as having been on the battlefield at San Jacinto. He was more needed there than back at Washington.

Although for days there had been much confusion with Santa Anna's large army on the move, it seemed that General Houston was in retreat, and many were becoming angered that they did not engage in a fight. Nothing more was needed to arouse the Texians. "Remember the Alamo; Remember Goliad!" was now the battle cry. And yet there seemed little they could do but run. The wiping out of the Texans at San Patricio, Agua Dulce, the Alamo, and Goliad had left the frontier without military protection. As Houston's army was retreating to the American frontier, as was popularly supposed, the panic ensued. Nothing stood between them, and the Mexican army and their panic could hardly be exaggerated.

The Runaway Scrape was in full force. Noah Smithwick, who later gave his firsthand account of this event, wrote in *Texas Yesterday and Today:*

> The desolation of the country through which we passed beggars description. Houses were standing open, the beds unmade, the breakfast things still on the tables, pan of milk molding in the dairies. There were cribs full of corn,

smokehouses full of bacon, yards full of chickens that ran after us for food, nests of eggs in every fence corner…hogs fat and lazy wallowing in the mud, all abandoned. Forlorn dogs roamed around the deserted homes, their doleful howls adding to the general sense of desolation. Hungry cats ran mewing to meet us…Wagons were so scarce that it was impossible to remove household good.

And, as if the arch fiend had broken loose, there were men—or devils, rather—bent on plunder, galloping up behind the fugitives, telling them the Mexicans were just behind, thus causing the hapless victims to abandon what few valuables they had tried to save. There were broken down wagons and household goods scattered all along the road. Stores with quite valuable stocks of goods stood open, the goods on the shelves, no attempt having been made to remove them.

At that point in time, the whole cause seemed lost. Had it not been for several miracles to occur, there would be no Republic of Texas. One of those miracles was Santa Anna taking the Texians too much for granted and letting his guard down.

## San Jacinto and Victory

A letter from General Sam Houston to David G. Burnet tells the story the best:

> Headquarters of the Army, San Jacinto,
> April 25, 1836
>
> To His Excellency, David G. Burnet, President of the Republic of Texas
>
> Sir: I regret extremely that my situation, since the battle of the 21st, has been such as to prevent my rendering you my official report of the same previous to this time.
>
> I have the honor to inform you that on the evening of the 18th inst., after a forced march of fifty-five miles,

the army arrived opposite Harrisburg. That evening a courier of the enemy was taken, from whom I learned that General Santa Anna, with one division of choice troops, had marched in the direction of Lynch's Ferry on the San Jacinto, burning Harrisburg as he passed down.

The army was ordered to be in readiness to march early on the next morning. The main body effected a crossing over Buffalo Bayou, below Harrisburg, on the morning of the 19th, having left the baggage, the sick, and a sufficient camp guard in the rear. We confirmed the march throughout the night, making but one halt in the prairie for a short time, and without refreshments. At daylight we resumed the line of march. In a short distance our scouts encountered those of the enemy, and we received information that General Santa Anna was at New Washington, and would that day take up the line of march for Anahuac, crossing at Lynch's Ferry. The Texian army halted within half a mile of the ferry in some timber and was engaged in slaughtering beeves, when the army of Santa Anna was discovered approaching in battle array.

About 9 o'clock on the morning of the 21st the enemy was reinforced by five hundred choice troops under the command of General Cos, increasing their effective force to upwards of fifteen hundred men, whilst our aggregate force for the field numbered seven hundred and eighty-three.

At half past 3 o'clock in the evening I ordered the officers of the Texian army to parade their respective commands, having in the meantime ordered the bridge on the only road communicating with the Brazos, distant eight miles from our encampment, to be destroyed, thus cutting off all possibility of escape. Our troops paraded with alacrity and spirit, and were anxious for the contest. The conscious disparity in numbers seemed only to increase their enthusiasm and confidence, and heighten their anxiety for the conflict.

Our cavalry was first dispatched to the front of the enemy's left, for the purpose of attracting notice, whilst an extensive island of timber afforded us an opportunity of concentrating our forces and deploying from that point. Every evolution was performed with alacrity, the whole advancing rapidly in line and through an open prairie, without any protection whatever for our men. The artillery advanced and took station within two hundred yards of the enemy's breastwork, and commenced an effective fire with grape and canister.

Colonel Sidney Sherman with his regiment having commenced the action upon our left wing, the whole line advancing in double-quick time, rung the war cry, "Remember the Alamo!" received the enemy's fire, and advanced within point blank shot before a piece was discharged from our lines.

The conflict lasted about eighteen minutes from the time of close action until we were in possession of the enemy's encampment. We took one piece of cannon (loaded), four stands of colors, all their camp equipage, stores, and baggage. Our cavalry had charged and routed that of the enemy upon the right, and given pursuit to the fugitives, which did not cease until they arrived at the bridge which I have mentioned. Captain Karnes, always the foremost in danger, commanded the pursuers. The conflict in the breastwork lasted but a few moments. Many of the troops encountered hand to hand, and not having the advantage of bayonets on our side, our riflemen used their pieces as war clubs, breaking many of them off at the breech.

The rout commenced at half past four, and the pursuit by the main army continued until twilight. A guard was then left in charge of the enemy's encampment and our army returned with their killed and wounded. In the battle our loss was two killed and twenty-three wounded, six of them mortally. The enemy's loss was six hundred and thirty killed; wounded, two hundred and eight; prisoners, seven hundred and thirty.

About six hundred muskets, three hundred sabres and two hundred pistols have been collected since the action. Several hundred mules and horses were taken, and near twelve thousand dollars in specie. For several days previous to the action our troops were engaged in forced marches, exposed to excessive rains, and the additional inconvenience of extremely bad roads, illy supplied with rations and clothing; yet amid every difficulty, they bore up with cheerfulness and fortitude, and performed their marches with spirit and alacrity. There was no murmuring.

For the commanding general to attempt discrimination as to the conduct of those who commanded in the action, or those who were commanded, would be impossible. Our success in the action is conclusive proof of such daring intrepidity and courage. Every officer and man proved himself worthy of the cause in which he battled, while the triumph received a lustre from the humanity which characterized their conduct after victory. Nor should we withhold the tribute of our grateful thanks from that Being who rules the destinies of nations, and has in the time of greatest need enabled us to arrest a powerful invader, whilst devastating our country.

I have the honor to be, with high consideration,

Your obedient servant,<br>Sam Houston, Commander-in-Chief

General Houston did not mention in this letter that he had been wounded. His horse had been shot out from under him, and he sustained a bullet wound in his leg. He also didn't mention how Santa Anna had been captured.

General Sam Houston

At the beginning of the battle, Santa Anna was in his tent with a woman and was literally caught with his pants down. He quickly had a regular soldier give him his clothing, and he fled. When the Texian army was rounding up the Mexican troops that had fled, three of them came upon one that was hiding. They debated on what to do with him but decided to march him back to camp. Immediately, Santa Anna was recognized by his own men when they entered camp. He was brought before General Houston and taken into custody. He was held captive for a while, but later, he was sent back to Mexico. That is a long story, and it is advised that the reader research Santa Anna for further information on this dictator.

The heroes of the Gonzales, the Alamo, Goliad, and San Jacinto have been documented and read about in countless books and vivid accounts of their bravery. Davy Crockett, William B. Travis, Jim Bowie, Sam Houston, and so many others have been written about over and over. Streets, schools, and towns have been named for the heroes of Texas history.

There are many unsung heroes in Texas history. Dr. Robert Peebles's heroic deeds have been recorded but never applauded, and yet if he had not taken the documents, deeds, and all the transactions from San Felipe, would the settlers still have been able to come back to their lands?

## Documentation of Dr. Peebles' Having Saved the Archives

This letter documents that Dr. Robert Peebles had taken the documents:

New Orleans June 23 d 1836

Dear Genl.

I write merely to say that the Acting President of the Govt., of Mexico, Jose Justo Carro, has determined to disregard the Armistice agreed upon between Genl Houston and St. Anna, and has issued his proclamation declaring his intention to prosecute the War against Texas immediately. Our Country, it seems by this publication, (which has been republished in the Bulletin of this City), is to be invaded by seventeen thousand Men. The prevailing opinion here is that Texas should loose no time in making ample preparation to repel the expected invasion: And acting under this impression the Citizens of Texas who have joined in a recommendation to Genl Hunt to proceed immediately with his preparations to raise and organize his Division, as you May see by the enclosed Copy. A report reached here today from Vera Cruz that the Gov was not able to raise the men and money to carry on another Campaign against us. I did not learn from what authority this report emanated, but it is only necessary for us to reflect how woefully the people of Texas have been lead astray by such idle rumors to lead us at once to the conclusion that now is the time to prepare for action.

> I leave in the morning for Mobile, thence to Claiborne, from whence I shall return with all possible dispatch. Please Write Me to San Augustine immediately upon the receipt of this, and if in your opinion the return of the Archives had better be delayed I will act upon your advice.
>
> I am much indisposed therefore Must Make My letter Short.
>
> R. Peebles

This letter was addressed to Gen. S. F. Austin, Quintanna, Texas.

> Citizens of Texas in New Orleans to Memucan Hunt
> June 23, 1836

The Texas Republic had begun, and the archives that Dr. Robert Peebles was to deliver would be an important part of the establishing the new republic.

# 4

# The Legacy of Stephen Fuller Austin

> Wherefore seeing we also are compassed about with so great a cloud of witnesses…let us run with patience the race that is set before us, looking unto Jesus the author and finisher of our faith.
>
> —Hebrews 12:1–2

Stephen Austin and the others in his colony had worked long and hard in their endeavors to colonize Texas. His close friends Gail Borden Jr., Dr. Robert Peebles, and a long list of others had worked tirelessly to achieve success. Samuel M. Williams was a close friend, but Austin had become troubled on hearing that his friend had betrayed him when he was in a Mexican prison. There would be exchanges of letters between Austin and Williams and the others on many occasions, which would tell the history of those days prior to Texas Independence and the months following.

In fact, Austin wrote hundreds of letters and received the same. The story of early Texas has been documented in those many letters. Austin was an excellent writer and expressed his feelings well to his friends, family, and often to just an acquaintance. The sum of those letters can easily comprise a very large book, but a few will tell the story of his legacy.

## Letter from Gail Borden

In 1833, the colonists had written a new constitution. It was decided that Austin would go to Mexico City to present the constitution and a list of other demands to the Mexican government. Austin was thrown into prison on suspicion of inciting an insurrection and the newly written constitution ignored. In August

1835, he was released but, upon his return to Texas, found that the Texans were on the brink of rebellion. There was nothing more he could do and began to prepare for war.

After the war, Austin wrote a letter to his friend W. S. Archer, dated August 15, 1836. He was at Peach Point Plantation near Velasco. W. S. Archer was a relative of Branch T. Archer, who had traveled to the United States with Austin during the fight for independence.

He wrote,

> The kind interest you take in the affairs of this Country, and the expression of your intentions to visit Texas next fall with the probable view of emigrating here is in the highest degree encouraging for it gives new life to hope, which I have long cherished, of seeing Texas populated with men who will bring to it such resources of experience, of wisdom, of virtue, and of mental treasures as well as of enterprise, and pecuniary wealth.

In this letter to Archer, he was describing his deepest feelings and desires for Texas.

> I consider that the foundation is laid—the superstructure is in progress, and is precisely in the stage when able architects are most needed. Texas is fully redeemed from the wilderness, and its independence is virtually achieved—this I call the foundation.

He revealed in this letter that he was in favor of annexation to the United States and hoped for that to happen by the spring of 1837. He also hoped that his friends would nominate him as a candidate for president of the Republic in the upcoming elections.

On August 15, 1836, Austin received the following letter from his good friend Gail Borden Jr.

Dear Genl.,

    I have but a few moments to write, but in these few, I wish to tell you that from the sign of the times you can not be elected, unless you or some friend comes out in a circular to the people. The lamented land speculation is operating against you. Many have been led to believe that you are concerned

    I have just returned from Fort Bend, and some of your old devoted friends say, they can not support you unless they are convinced that you had no hand in the big land purchase. They say, if you will tell them you have not, they will believe you.

    It is easy for your enemies to make use of this vile plea to ruin your election. It is necessary, therefore, that something should be said on this subject. I know how much this affair has tormented your soul, and it is due to yourself as well as to the public that you make a positive denial of having anything to do with what is called land speculation. I have, when speaking of this affair offered to pledge my life on the question; that is, I would give my life, if at any time it should be found that you were engaged in the affair.

    Let us know what you wish done and believe me.

Of course, Borden knew who the land speculators had been and one of them, Dr. Robert Peebles, had in his possession all the archives of the land deals that had been made. As mentioned in an earlier chapter, Samuel Williams and Frank Johnson had been in on the land speculations with Dr. Peebles.

Austin replied to Borden's letter:

> I have just received your letter of the 15$^{th}$ instant, informing me that great efforts are making to circulate reports and slanders, for the purpose of injuring me, at the election which is to be held on the first Monday of the next month. Such things are to be expected. In all communities, there are men, who attempt to rise and effect their individual

views, by trying to mislead the public. The check upon them, is the good sense and sound judgment of the people. Relying upon this check, I have not considered it necessary to notice any of the slang that has been circulated about me.

I feel but little anxiety, of a personal character, whether I am elected or not. I am not a volunteer candidate, for I agreed to become one from a sense of duty, because I was solicited to do so, by persons whose opinions I could not disregard, without laying myself liable, at least in some degree, to the imputation of having shrunk from a high and responsible station, at a time when the situation of Texas was most critical, and its political affairs most difficulty. Had I refused being a candidate, I should then have been censured for abandoning, in the time of difficulty, the public affairs of a country, to which I have devoted so many years to build up and bring forward.

## Time in the Mexican Prison

That letter to Borden went on for pages as Austin reiterates to his friend, who already knew all this, of his service to Texas. The letter, and others he wrote, attested to the anguish he was feeling. The fact he was ill and very tired only added to his concerns. In this letter, he details his time in a Mexican prison.

> In April, 1833, I was appointed by the people of Texas, represented in general convention, to go to the city of Mexico as their agent or commissioner, to apply for the admission of Texas into the Mexican confederation as a State. This appointment was ruinous to my individual interests, and in every respect hazardous and fatiguing. I accepted it, however, from a sense of duty and went to Mexico at my individual expense, for I never asked, or received one dollar from the country for that trip. I was imprisoned in Mexico, as is well known, and detained about two years. During this time, it seems that some persons

engaged in large land speculations at Monclova, the seat of government of the state of Coahuila and Texas. These are the speculations to which you allude in your letter of the 15th instant, and which, you say, are ruinous to my election. You ask me what man has labored with purer intentions, or with a more ardent and disinterested desire to promote the prosperity, and happiness, and liberty of Texas, and I will also say, that I consented to become a candidate at this election with great reluctance. I have been absent from Texas, a public business, for about three years. During this time, my individual affairs have been neglected, and much of the old colonizing business remained unclosed. It was my wish and intention to devote this year to those objects, at the same time giving all the aid I could, as a citizen, to the public cause.

He ended the letter, saying it was a long response to Borden's reply to his letter. He felt it necessary to write all those feelings. He would express himself many more times of his concerns in letters and would receive letters of encouragement and offers of help in the new Republic of Texas.

## Letter from Samuel M. Williams

On August 29, 1836, came a letter from New Orleans. Samuel M. Williams had heard from sources that his good friend Austin was deeply dissatisfied with his former dealings and betrayals.

The letter was written from New Orleans, August 1836. Williams wrote, "If any single expression of mine in this letter should wound or mortify your feelings I entreat you…I would not on you inflict the wound you have given me." Williams had felt he didn't deserve the charges made by Austin and was now denying them.

It was a long letter wherein Williams declared his allegiance to his friend Austin and would hope for a response. He wished him well in running for president, confirming that in "this country," it would be well received.

> It will tend very much to give character and confidence to our new institutions—and God grant you may succeed.

Williams had good reason to write a letter in that he had been accused of dealings that were not intentioned to be bad for Texas. In 1823, Austin had first hired Williams as a translator and clerk at San Felipe de Austin. In the fall of 1824, Austin appointed Williams as a recording secretary for the Austin Colony. He managed the Public Land Office, and he served as its postmaster from 1826. He served as secretary of the *ayuntamiento* from 1828 to 1832, a post requiring him to record official documents in Spanish and send them to the state government.

Austin later claimed that Williams had been underpaid for his service and later compensated him with 49,000 acres of land in Texas. With his existing land grant of 9,387 acres, Williams had accumulated more than 58,000 acres of land in Texas.

Early in 1834, he cofounded the partnership of McKinney and Williams, setting up a warehouse at Brazoria, then relocated to Quintana, at the mouth of the Brazos River. The firm operated small steamboats on the Brazos and used its warehouse to manage transfer of freight to and from the larger ships operating on the Gulf of Mexico.

Williams bought one hundred leagues of land in northeast Texas from the Monclova government at an 80 percent discount. During the trip, he also secured a bank charter while selling $85,000 worth of its stock. However, in November 1835, the Consultation nullified the land deal when it declared all large land grants voided. This was the land deal that Frank Johnson and Dr. Robert Peebles had been in on. This could not be held against these men as the deal was voided.

In 1835, he represented the Brazos district in the Coahuila and Texas Legislature. Later in the year, he was branded a revolutionary for raising funds to oppose Santa Anna, at which point he moved back to the United States. Williams was selling bank stock in New York when he read about a possible war in Texas. He borrowed against his brother's credit to obtain the 125-ton schooner *Invincible* on behalf of the Texian rebels. In May of 1836, Williams returned with ammunition and supplies loaded on his schooner, as well as many as seven hundred volunteers on three other boats. Mostly as a result of procurements Williams made in the United States in 1835, the McKinney's and William's partnership had contracted $99,000 in short-term debt on behalf of the Republic of Texas. The new government was not able to repay the debt.

Williams, as had many of Austin's close friends, sacrificed much for the Republic of Texas. In the letters written during the time after the Independence from Mexico had been won, Austin didn't refer to or may not have realized just how much his friends had done for Texas. He never accused Dr. Peebles or any others of wrongdoing but lambasted Williams.

## The New Government of the Republic of Texas

After gaining their independence and not wasting much time, the Texas voters had elected a Congress of fourteen senators and twenty-nine representatives in September 1836. The Constitution allowed the first president to serve for two years and the subsequent presidents for three years. Sam Houston had been elected by popular vote to the office of president. Although Austin had run for the office, he would lose with the least amount of votes. Henry Smith, another candidate for the office, had gotten more votes, which seemed to confirm that some Texans no longer trusted Austin. More likely, the reason was that Sam Houston was the hero having defeated Santa Anna at San Jacinto.

The second Congress of the Republic of Texas convened in October 1836 at Columbia (now West Columbia). Mirabeau B. Lamar was the vice president, and Houston appointed Austin as the secretary of state. By that appointment, Houston showed that he trusted Austin explicitly, and he was certain his friend was the perfect choice.

In 1836, five sites had served as temporary capitals of Texas. Washington, where the delegates met to sign the Declaration of Independence, had been the first. A temporary capitol was at Harrisburg, following the defeat of Santa Anna, as that is where the ad interim president had taken refuge during the conflict. Galveston was briefly the capitol, then Velesco, with a decision by the newly elected congress choosing Columbia. It wasn't much of a capital, having a rundown building barely big enough to house the government of the new Texas Republic. Later, President Sam Houston moved the capital to Houston in 1837. After some debate, the Texas Capitol finally came to be at Austin.

## Austin's Letters to Others

His letters begin to tell of his grave concerns and illness. In September 1836, Gail Borden Jr. wrote the following letter addressed to General S. F. Austin, Peach Point:

Columbia 19th—Sept. 1836

Dear Friend,
    Yours of this date is before me and I hasten to answer.

    I am this moment been informed by Capt. Baker that Drs. Miller and Peebles have returned from Nacogdoches, the latter having brought on the public papers—What is going to be done with them—I presume however, he will keep them till the meeting of Congress.

    If Congress is held at this place a room will be very difficult to obtain for the present. I am in hopes, however you can have an opportunity to look over and regulate the papers—it would have been done before if I had had a Spanish scholar—You can now be accommodated by Austin B and Mr. Gritton—Mr. Gritton can do more business in the Spanish than any person I know of.

Austin will answer every purpose. Aunt Mary is at present very unwell, and not able to sit up. You ask how she could be got down? I could send her in the Steam boat to any point you wish on the Brazos—please inform me where.

I regret much to hear of your ill health, hope you will soon be restored, and come up. I will do every thing in my power to assist you with the papers, but Austin Must help

In haste your friend
G. Borden, Jr.

Austin had resided in a small building in San Felipe prior to the Revolution. It was burned to the ground with the other structures after most of his personal items and papers were removed by his friend Dr. Robert Peebles, which he had taken to Louisiana for safekeeping. Austin was residing at Peach Point Plantation for the most part.

In the spring of 1836, Austin, Dr. Branch T. Archer, and William H. Wharton had traveled through the United States, giving speeches and arousing sympathy for Texas. A company of volunteers was raised at Lexington, Kentucky, but it had reached Texas several months after the battle of San Jacinto, when it was no longer needed. The authorities could do nothing, of course, but thank them and send them back home. On their return to Lexington, Colonel Wilson and Captain Postlewaite declared that they had been treated badly by the Texans. The following letter written by Austin addresses some of those concerns. This letter illustrates some of the hardships he suffered for the sake of Texas:

My Dear Sir: I have received several letters from you, and I fear that you have accused me of neglect in not answering them sooner. As an Apology, I have to say that on my arrival at Velasco on June 29 I was called up the country on important business, and was in motion during the whole of July and August. The last of August I was taken sick with fever at the headquarters of the army, and with difficulty reached this place (the residence of my brother-in-law, Mr. James F. Perry). I have had a severe attack, but am now convalescent, though dyspeptic to a great degree, and so debilitated that I am barely able to get about.

I have been told that I have been accused of not treating our Lexington friends with sufficient attention. This has mortified me very much, for I do not merit it. I have no house, not a roof in all Texas, that I can call my own. The only one I had was burnt at San Felipe during the late invasion of the enemy. I make my home where the business of the country calls me. There is none here at the farm of my brother-in-law. He only began to open up the place three years ago and is still in the primitive log cabins and the shrubbery of the forest.

I have no farm, no cotton plantation, no income, no money, no comforts. I have spent the prime of my life and worn out my constitution in trying to colonize this country. Many persons boast of their three or four hundred leagues, acquired by speculation without personal labor or the sacrifice of years or even days. I shall be content to save twenty leagues, or about ninety thousand acres, acquired very hardly and very dearly, indeed.

All my wealth is prospective and contingent upon events of the future. What I have been able from time to time to realize in active means has gone as fast as realized, and much faster, for I am still in debt for the expenses of my trip to Mexico in 1833, 1834, and 1835. My health and strength and time have gone in the service to Texas, and I am therefore not ashamed of my present poverty.

I deeply, most deeply regret that any difficulty or dissatisfaction should have occurred with the volunteers.

It is a misfortune but it ought not and certainly can not injure the cause of this country.

Please remember me to my old friends. I hope before March the United States flag will wave all over Texas. God grant it may.

Yours most truly,<br>S. F. Austin

The anguish that Austin felt over his health, lack of funds, and property is expressed most profoundly in this letter. Why, in the last paragraph, his hope to see the United States flag wave over Texas is not clear. It was a Republic, a country, and its own flag was already waving. He also expressed a bit of disdain for persons who had three or four hundred leagues of land through speculation as his friends in San Felipe had engaged in that practice, including Dr. Peebles.

On October 12, 1836, Austin writes a most damning letter to Samuel Williams. In that letter, he accuses his friend unmercifully, and here are some of the accusations:

> I read your letter with such feelings as a drowning man would seize a plank—Sam Williams you were wound around and rooted in my affections more than any man ever was or ever can be again—I wished and hoped to see or hear something that would convince me I was wrong or had too seriously viewed your acts etc. since I left in 1833. You were to have closed the land business pending of the old colonies and attended to the last one—nothing was done or next to nothing, and I still have all that cursed trouble on my hands besides the censure and Gabble of discontent, which is of little consequence it is true but is not very pleasant—But all this is nothing, those cursed Monclova speculations and Contracts by which you have involved yourself and friends and country in evils which will last for years, and which you certainly never even drempt of and know nothing of now—W. H. Jack was the man

who gave me the first account of that damned transaction that I understood. That an attempt was made by you to get up an excitement in the Colony and to draw men from here under the pretext of defending the Governor, when in reality they were to be used as a part of the pay you and others were to be given on one of those contracts—I was led and bound to believe by Jack's statement; and also that you spared no kind of pains to precipitate the country into war immediately, and event which you must have known would have perpetuated my imprisonment indefinitely—you also must have known that all the odium of those things, would be cast on me by the envious and slanderous owing to our long friendship and relations. The fact is Williams that all those Monclova matters, I mean the speculations, and precipitating the country into war, were morally wrong, they have some very criminal and dreadful features—I am too much debilitated to say more you say your motives were good—IN the name of God convince me of that—Had I cared nothing about you and McKinney these things would have had no effect on me. McKinney began abusing and slandering me when I was absent in the U. S. his idea of friendship is that one must be the tool of his friend right or wrong—he has chosen his course and is quite welcome to keep it—he is very far from being the high minded man I once believed him to be—But you will probably get on well—Speculation and honesty cannot contend in Texas the former will gain some twenty or 100 to one. What I mean by honesty here is honesty to the public interest and the public good—convince me in the name of God that you have been and are honest to the public interest and the public good as you say you have been and restore yourself where you once stood in the opinion of S. F. Austin.

Austin confirmed in a letter that Dr. Peebles had taken the archives to safety:

> Columbia, Oct. 22, 1836
>
> Hons. S. H. Everett, Chairman of the Com. Of the senate on pub. Lands
>
> Sir,
> I have just rec d—your official note dated yesterday, informing me of the resolution of the senate, requesting all Empresarios to make a report of their contracts of colonization, proceedings under them etc. etc.
>
> Believing that it was my duty to make a report of the character required by the senate, I should have done so, at the meeting of congress, without waiting for a special call, but the absence of all the land records and papers, and my own absence from Texas on public service, most of the time since 1833, rendered it impossible.
>
> Dr. Peebles, who had charge of the land records during the invasion, has now gone to bring them to this place, and the report called for will be presented as soon as it can be made out.
>
> I must observe that this report will necessarily embrace everything connected with colonization, so far as I have been concerned, and will comprehend a period of about fifteen years. It therefore will require great labor and much time to complete it. My ill health I fear will cause some delay. I however assure you that ever effort will be made on my part to finish it as soon as possible, and in the mean time any information in my power to give to the committee will be cheerfully afforded.
>
> I have the honor to remain your most obedient servant.
>
> S. F. Austin

In early October 1836, Dr. Robert Peebles had returned to Texas with the archives he had taken from the courthouse in San Felipe. He delivered the documents, all papers, and records, including the evidence of his own illegal transactions, to Austin at Peach Point Plantation. Those illegal transactions were dismissed as stated above. Dr. Peebles and the others were never prosecuted for illegal transactions.

The letters that Austin was writing took much of his time but are detailed accounts of so much of what was happening in his life. On October 21, 1836, he wrote to S. H. Everett, chairman of the Committee of the Senate on public lands.

> Sir, I have just rec'd your official note dated yesterday, informing me of the resolution of the senate, requesting all Empresarios to make a report of their contracts of colonization proceedings under them, etc. etc.
>
> Believing that it was my duty to make a report of the character required by the senate, I should have done so, at the meeting of congress, without waiting for a special call, but the absence of all the land records and papers, and my own absence from Texas on public service, most of the time since 1833, rendered it impossible.
>
> Dr. Peebles, who had charge of the land records during the invasion has now gone to bring them to this place, and the report called for will be presented as soon as it can be made out—I must observe that this report will necessarily embrace every thing connected with colonization, so far as I have been concerned, and will comprehend a period of about fifteen years. It therefore will require great labor and much time to complete it. My ill health I fear will cause some delay, I however assure you that every effort will be made on my part to finish it as soon as possible, and in the mean time any information in my power to give to the committee will be cheerfully afforded.

## Austin's Last Letter to Houston

Austin seemed almost obsessed with writing letters and wrote well into the evening. He seemed to know he had little time to get all of what was required of him in place. Plus, in his letters, he was telling his side of the story.

On October 31, 1836, he wrote a letter to President Sam Houston.

> To his Excellency Genl. Sam Houston
> President of the republic of Texas
>
> Sir,
>
> I have the honor to acknowledge the receipt of your Excellency's official letter of 28th instant informing me that the senate had confirmed my nomination to the office of Secretary of State, and requesting me to say whether I accept of said appointment—Your Excellency is fully aware of the debilitated state of my constitution and health, and also of the labors which devolve upon me in the land department. I however accept of the appointment and am ready to enter upon the duties of the office, with the understanding that I be allowed the privilege of retiring should my health and situation require it.
>
> I have the honor to present to your Excellency the assurances of my high respect and to remain your Excellency's
>
> S. F. Austin.

## Final Letter to Samuel Williams

One more letter from Austin to Samuel Williams came from the Williams Papers at the Rosenberg library in Galveston, Texas. It is included here because of its profound significance to their friendship and the pain that these friends had caused one another.

Austin to S. M. Williams
Columbia Novr. 3 1836

This is my birthday—my health is much improved tho still bad and I am still tormented with dyspepsia, a most cursed disease, for body and mind—the public matters are getting on well—the state of things, which I have long labored to bring about is gradually coming around, which is union and the disappearance of those old parties and nonsense which in times past have distracted and almost ruined this country—I believe that I have contributed something towards bringing about this state of things—tho at the loss perhaps of some men who called themselves old friends I am as rapidly as I can gradually preparing to relieve myself in toto from all kinds of public business and shall do so permanently as soon as I can.

Come home Williams and lay aside your wild mode of talking about the people and everything else—it is tie for you to stop all that kind of wildness both in talking, acts and business—harm enough has been done already by it—do no more—you have greatly vexed and worried and distressed me. So much so that my brain has been greatly fevered. I am in a considerable degree getting over it—It is no easy matter to admit anything like permanent estrangement from a person who has been united to us by close friendship for years and in times of trouble you have done wrong and have greatly injured your friends, yourself, and our country—but that is past—let it be a lesson to you for the future—come home—the land affairs are to be closed and reported to congress by 1 of December—I wish to get rid of it all as soon as possible and wash my hands of it all forever.

As to yourself—let politics and the public affairs alone—arrange your past business—get a standing with the cotton planters, and confine yourself exclusively to commercial business—the purchase of cotton and sale of goods will present a vast field to a regular merchant who has no other "iron in the fire"—but the old farmers are suspicious and watchful—they like a safe merchant, and not one who does business on a dashing or gambling scale. I repeat the remarks in substance I made to you in a letter from Mexico when I first heard you were going into the mercantile business, and had you been governed by them more closely than you have been you would have saved much loss and difficulty and injury and mortification to your friends, and to me in particular—That cursed Monclova trip of yours has indeed been a curse to you and to me and to the country and to everyone else. I am trying to banish even the recollection of it from my mind, and when I fully recover my health, hope shall be able to do so. In future I never mean to speak of it or allude to it, if I can avoid it—I have cursed it in so many forms and shapes that my anger is becoming almost exhausted and will, I sincerely hope, finally wear away. Williams you have wounded me very deeply, buy you are so deeply rooted in my affections, that with all your faults, you are at heart too much like a wild and heedless brother to be entirely banished. Come home. Your old friend

S. F. Austin

Austin had poured out his heart in that letter to Williams. One wonders how Williams took it and if he felt unjustly accused. He had expressed to Austin in a previous letter that he was hurt by the accusations. One more time, Austin lambasts his friend but pleads with him to come home. He didn't express himself in that way to any of the other men who were involved in the land speculations.

## Santa Anna's Letter to Austin

On November 5, 1836, Austin received a letter from Santa Anna. In that letter, he wrote of the desire of the Texians for annexation into the United States. As secretary of state, Austin would have been the one to whom Santa Anna would address his desire to facilitate going to what he called "Washington City." He wanted Austin to facilitate his journey to Washington with the least possible delay.

Santa Anna's conclusion of the letter was one of a complete narcissistic personality:

> I conclude by repeating to you what I have said in writing and verbally—that my name already known to the world—shall not be tarnished by any unworthy action; Gratitude is characteristic of me—consequently you will have nothing on our part to repent of.
>
> To you I owe my existence, and various other favors which are deeply impressed on me—and which I will endeavor to reciprocate as the so justly merit.

The first congress of the Republic of Texas had assembled at Columbia on the Brazos in October, and the fate of the captive president was a great theme that was debated in both houses. The leaders in congress were in favor of Santa Anna's execution, and if the matter had been left to a vote, he would have lost. President Houston was a man of great firmness and had determined to spare the life of the Mexican dictator as being "the political thing to do."

Andrew Jackson, president of the United States, had written to Houston, urging that he be released. In November, while the congressmen at Columbia were debating the fate of the "illustrious prisoner," President Houston cut the debate short by sending Santa Anna to "Washington City" with an escort. They left the Brazos on November 25, 1836.

## Austin at Peach Point Plantation

Peach Point Plantation was the home of James Franklin Perry and his wife, Emily Austin Bryan Perry, the sister of Stephen F.

Austin. The plantation is situated between Jones Creek and the Brazos River, ten miles south of Brazoria on State Highway 36. It was named by Austin for the wild peach trees growing there. Of all the property in his colony, Peach Point was Austin's first choice for a home site. Soon after his sister's family had arrived in Texas on August 14, 1831, Austin drew up suggested plans for the Perry's home. In the construction of Peach Point, Perry had followed a number of Austin's suggestions about materials and design of the residence. In accordance with his later instructions, two rooms built at the east end of the house were set aside for his use as a bedroom and office.

The letter from Austin to James Perry from Victoria was dated September 2, 1836:

> Dr Brother (the Dr, meant Dear)
> I am still here. Archer is on the mend and I think will be able to travel in a few days in a wagon down to the landing where he can embark—I shall proceed home—my own health is not very good, tho I have no severe attack of fever.
> I wrote you the other day, requesting that you would put up a cabbin with two rooms for me, or if lumber and workmen can be had, a frame—the log house perhaps will be the easiest, and quickest—I need one room for an office or sitting room, and one for a sleeping room.
> I must make your house my home for a time say until spring at least, and wish to devote the winter to closing and arranging all my business—I must have one clerk at least, and perhaps two and there ought to be three rooms, one for a sleeping room for the clerks and visitors.
> I also wish you to make out an order on N. Orleans for the necessary mattresses, chairs, tables etc. unless they can be had without sending there.
> I can sell some land and have the money ready for these purposes and for all the necessary supplies of provisions etc. The sooner you can get workmen and put up the cabbin

etc. the better—it must have a shingle roof with extended eves so as to keep the wet from driving in etc.—I wish to get Joseph Baker to assist in closing the land business.

These arrangements are made on the supposition that I shall not be elected—Houston will, I am told, get all the east, and Red River now—Many of the old settlers who are too blind to see or understand their interest will vote for him, and the army I believe will go for him, at least the majority of them—So that I have a good prospect of some rest this year, and time to regulate my private affairs, which need regulating very much.

S. F. Austin

In this letter, it is clearly evident that Austin knew he would not be elected president, which seemed to be a relief for him. He was tired from travels, and he was ill.

Other letters to his brother-in-law showed that Austin was eager to come back to Peach Point. He was already planning what trees to plant and what to build.

The plantation went through prosperous times during the Republic and early statehood. It was visited in January 1848 by Rutherford B. Hayes, a classmate of Emily Perry's son, Guy M. Bryan. During the Civil War and Reconstruction, Peach Point, like other Texas plantations, declined sharply in productivity and profitability, and much of the land was sold to satisfy debts. Discovery of oil on the property in the 1930s brought better times, and some of the original land was bought back by S. S. Perry Sr. With the exception of the two rooms set aside for Austin's use, the plantation house was destroyed by a hurricane in 1909. By 1948, those two rooms had deteriorated badly, but painstaking restoration of these rooms were undertaken and are now furnished primarily with original Austin and Perry family heirlooms.

Peach Point as it looked prior to the hurricane

# 5

## Stephen Fuller Austin
## Father of Texas

> The prosperity of Texas has been the object of my labors, the idol of my existence; it has assumed the character of a religion for the guidance of my thoughts and actions of fifteen years, superior to all pecuniary or personal views.
>
> —Stephen Fuller Austin

## Austin's Final Days

As sick as he was, Austin had returned to Columbia to begin the task of secretary of state for the New Republic of Texas. He was staying in the home of George B. McKinstry, which was located a few miles from Columbia. When he was at the McKinstry home, he was at the capital building, staying up late into the night, writing.

He had been ill ever since his stay in the Mexican prison. The stress of the war, the travels to the United States, and then his duties as secretary of state had proven to be too much for his weak constitution. He became ill with a cold and then pneumonia. On Christmas Eve, Austin had taken to bed with a chill and sank quickly into a fever and delirium.

In 1844, Guy M. Bryan, nephew to Austin, had written to George Hammeken, wanting details of the death of his uncle. Hammeken had been with Austin when he died. Hammeken had met Austin in Mexico City in 1833 and had come to know Austin well, although he had never lived in Texas. Austin had urged him to come to Texas and live, but he always refused. Although he was originally from New York State, he went to Mexico and stayed. Eventually, he married a Mexican woman.

He wrote to Guy Bryan about a comment made by Austin,

> Hammeken, if they had let me alone, I would have had 200,000 inhabitants in Texas, before attempting a separation from Mexico.

He continued,

> It is essential, to elucidate one of the main questions of your uncle's life, that all possible light should be thrown on his ulterior view with regard to Texas. His foresight, for which he was remarkable, arising from the good sense, which was the principal ingredient of his character, must have led him to the conclusion that at some future time two races, so dissimilar in every point of view as are the citizens of the United States and of Mexico, must come into collision, but at the same time he knew that as long as Mexico could be lulled, Texas would advance in strength and prosperity.

While Austin was imprisoned in Mexico at the dungeons of Ex-Inquisition, Hammeken had tried to visit his friend but was told Austin was not to be spoken to. He was moved to Acordada, another prison, and his friends were allowed to see him as often as they liked. Hammeken went to him often to converse with him and carry him books, thus becoming close friends.

Hammeken devised a plan of escape from Acordada when it was reported that Austin might be banished for ten years to California. Austin was in agreement with the plan but would not escape as long as there was a chance of being cleared. Fortunately, Austin was removed to the Diputacion prison. At that time, a general amnesty law for all political offences passed the Mexican Congress. This procured his release, and he left Mexico City on July 13, 1835.

Hammeken wrote to Bryan that he had seen his uncle in New Orleans in January 1836. They walked together down Canal

Street and talked of the strife with Mexico. Hammeken offered that perhaps paying Mexico millions of dollars could avoid a conflict. Austin assured him that if that were the case and he had the authority, he would do what he could to avoid a conflict, but he doubted anything could be arranged before blood was shed in Texas.

Hammeken had some influence with Mexican General Barragán. Upon his return to Mexico that January, he was to discuss the possibility of avoiding a conflict with Texas with the General. Barragán had traveled extensively in the United States and had a high opinion of Americans. He was benevolent and humane and also possessed a considerable influence with Santa Anna. General Barragán was on his deathbed, and the whole scheme that Hemmeken had devised was defeated before it began.

Hammeken saw General Austin again in New Orleans in June 1836. He had heard previously of Barragán's death. They left for Texas together on the steamboat *Union*. Austin went to see Santa Anna, who was in captivity at that time.

They rode together to Peach Point Plantation, where Hammeken copied sundry letters for him. These were letters to President Jackson, General Gaines, and a letter to Santa Anna from Jackson. Hammeken wrote to Bryan that he should have copies of those letters. Today these most important copies are in the Austin Collection of the University of Texas.

The letter written to Austin's nephew, Guy Bryan from George Hammeken, is one of the most significant pieces of history of Austin's last years and his dealings with Mexico. Hammeken gives a firsthand account in detail so that there is no question of his friendship with General Austin and of those events he wrote about.

Hammeken had not been to what he called home in five years. He went to New York and returned in December, 1836. He went shortly after his arrival to see his friend at Columbia where, as noted in the recollections of his letter to Austin's nephew, Guy Bryan, "I found General Austin on a sick bed."

> "Well, Hammeken, I am glad to see you. What do you think of going about? We'll give you some place in the government, and I'll let you have some of my stock—they say, it will be very valuable."
>
> Hammeken replied that he did not want any place. He went on to write, "in Mexico he had told me his private affairs were greatly deranged in consequence of his attention to public matters, and if he chose, I would aid him in arranging his own affairs."

Austin said that would suit him exactly and that when he got better, they would talk more about it. From that time, the afternoon of Friday, December 23, Hammeken was at Austin's bedside.

Austin's severe cold a week prior would have been for a person in good health of no consequence. He was, as the physicians attending him assured Hammeken, not of sound constitution, which anyone who knew Austin could ascertain. On Saturday, the 24th his condition had improved, but it was still grave.

"I found him somewhat stupefied from the effects of the opium they had given him, and conversed but little with him that evening. On the following morning he appeared much relieved, and told me that it gave him satisfaction to converse," he wrote of his dear friend.

The next day was Sunday and Christmas morning. He seemed so much better that Captain Henry Austin, his cousin, advised him to be shaved and have his linen changed. They brought him out of the little room where his bed had been enclosed with clapboards, very open and without a fireplace or a stove. He was placed on a pallet before the fire. That was in the morning, and the weather had been very mild and pleasant. As it often happens in Texas, at about 10:00 a.m., a strong northern wind came blowing in, and it turned very cold. They put him to bed again on his request.

Shortly after he was in bed, two papers were brought to him for his signature—the one Capt. Henry Austin read and the other what Hammeken read. They both agreed that General Austin should not sign either of the papers in his present condition and told him so. "What is the nature of them?" he asked.

"I told him that they would compromise his whole estate, and further remarked that I did not recollect ever asking a favor from him, but that now I would take it as a great favor if he would not at that time sign these papers."

Taking the advice of his longtime and trusted friend, Austin did not sign them.

Hammeken immediately went out and told the bearer, Dr. Branch Archer, that General Austin, by the advice of his friends, would not at that time sign papers of so much importance as to compromise his whole estate. The doctor remarked, "It is no more that I have done. I have compromised my whole estate, and he must either sign or relinquish his interest."

General Austin was told of Archer's words. "Let him draw out the relinquishment," was his only reply. He was weak and conversed with great effort. The relinquishment was signed that same day, and he became much worse that evening.

On Monday, James Perry, Austin's brother-in-law was sent for. At that time, others in the Congress were apprised of his condition. Columbia, the capitol of the Republic, was on alert that the great statesman and secretary of state, Stephen F. Austin, was critically ill.

In the afternoon, Dr. Levi Jones and Dr. Leger, the attending physicians, held a consultation and differed on treatment for the gravely ill patient. Jones wished to administer an Emetic, which was an expectorate to remove the phlegm that choked him. Leger opposed that method with the reasoning that Austin was so exhausted, his strength would fail him when he wanted to throw up the phlegm. Jones observed that if he did not take it, he would die in two hours. They referred to Hemmeken as to what he thought.

"I had no alternative—if he did not take Emetic, he would certainly die, although his life might, by not taking it, last a few hours more. I therefore requested Dr. Jones to give him the Emetic and whilst it was preparing Dr. Leger observed to me that he had changed his mind and felt it was his only chance."

They commenced with the ipecac, which failed to produce any other effect than to make him strain and weaken himself still more. He was then given Tartar Emeti, which had the desired effect. He breathed easier, but his strength was almost entirely gone. The doctors advised that he get some sleep, but he passed the night without closing his eyes for a moment. He would at times leave his bed and sit on a chair with his arms resting on a small table before him, with his head buried in his arms. This position seemed to be agreeable to him than the bed, but his weakness kept him from being able to stay in a sitting position for long. He arose, laid down several times during that long night as he passed from the room adjoining his bedroom to a pallet before the fire.

At daybreak, Austin's brother-in-law, James Perry and nephew, Austin Bryan arrived. At that time, Austin had become perfectly sensible. He immediately recognized them and expressed to them how happy he was to see them. They were told that there was no hope of his recovery.

At about 9:00 a.m., Dr. Leger applied blister to his chest, an archaic medical method to remove an infection. He knew it was to no avail but may have been administered at request of his family as an attempt to save Austin. Afterward, Austin said, "Now I will go to sleep." His left elbow was on his leg and his cheek resting on his hand, he seemed to be more at ease. His nephew was on his right, also supporting him.

Austin would, at intervals, ask for a little tea. During one of those intervals, he uttered his last words in a faint voice, which were distinctly understood by Austin and Hammeken:

"Texas recognized. Archer told me so. Did you see it in the papers?"

In about a half hour afterward, he ceased to breathe in the presence of James Perry, Dr. Branch Archer, and Austin Bryan.

To Guy Bryan, Hammeken wrote,

> I have now concluded my melancholy task. If your uncle had been spared for a few years longer, I would, by my attention to his business, probably have learned from himself many particulars relating to his life which would interest you. Those which I possess I have written with much prolixity, in order to help my memory as I proceeded. If you can cull out as many lines as I have written pages, I shall be most amply repaid. You may rely on the truth of all I have written; for I would not set down that of which I was not positive and certain. Should I at some future period revisit Mexico, in either a public or private capacity, it will afford me much pleasure to aid you in collecting material for your uncle's life. I left many friends there, and by their influence could have access to many State papers.

## Austin's Last Words and Preparations for His Funeral

About noon of the December 27, 1836, he raised from his pallet next to the fireplace and proclaimed, "Texas is recognized! Did you see it in the papers?" He fell back and was dead.

Upon hearing of Austin's death, President Sam Houston said to those gathered at the Capital, "The father of the Texas is no more! The first pioneer of the wilderness has departed! General Stephen F. Austin, Secretary of State, expired this day."

He continued to say that because of "his high standing, undeviated moral rectitude, his untiring zeal and valuable service," there would be a thirty-day period of mourning, with all civil and military officers to wear black crepe on their right arms and every post and garrison to fire a twenty-three gun salute—one for each county in the republic.

Austin's body lay in state at the Capital for two days. There was a steady procession of people from all around who came to view the body. As the word spread, the people of the Republic of Texas mourned for the man with whom they had come to know so well.

A special order went out as The Father of Texas, Stephen Fuller Austin is to be buried at Peach Point Plantation.

Columbia, 28, Dec 1836

> Immediately on receipt of the order you will detail a firing party to be commanded by yourself in person of (16) sixteen men with 4 rounds of blank cartridges to land over the Bayou above the house of McKinney and Williams and march immediately to the Residence of James F. Perry Esq. Should this order reach you in the night you (will) not fail to march forthwith—By order of his Excelly.

Geo. W. Poe

Dear Sir

> Hereweith you have an official order—uniform your men as the President will be there and show him how prompt you are in your duty—March the men to Perry's immediately tho' in the night you must get a guide have your men picked and in the neatest trim possible."

You will see me there—P

## The Yellowstone Steamboat

Austin's body was transported down the Brazos aboard the steamboat *Yellowstone* to Crosby's Landing, thence to the Perry family cemetery at Peach Point Plantation. A bill of lading exists, which is in the Brazoria County courthouse in Angleton, Texas. It shows the charges for shipment of the body to be $20 and passengers to be $4. The expenses were billed to the estate of Stephen F. Austin.

Many notables were aboard the steamboat that day, and it had not been the first time the *Yellowstone* had been used for such an important mission. It was only fitting that it would take Austin to his burial.

In late March and early April 1836, despite three Mexican forces under Santa Anna, Antonio Gaona, and Jose Urrea all searching for the Texas army along the right bank of the Brazos River, the *Yellowstone* steamed upstream to continue collecting cotton from the growers. In early April, Santa Anna was camped at San Felipe de Austin, fifteen miles below the yet undiscovered Texas camp near Groce's Landing, while General Gaona was marching southward down the brazos from the San Antonio Road, leaving the Texans caught in between.

On April 2, Sam Houston sent word to the *Yellowstone* to remain at Groce's Landing and prepare to assist in crossing the Texas Army. On April 12, the *Yellowstone* began crossing the entire Texas Army, completing the crossing with multiple trips by midafternoon the following day. On April 14, as the Texans marched toward San Jacinto, the *Yellowstone*, still armored in cotton bales, began her sprint downstream to pass the Mexican camps on her way to the Gulf. With her bell clanging and smoke billowing, the Yellowstone sent many of the Mexican soldiers running in fear, having never known the existence of such a craft as a steamboat.

Soon after the Texan's victory at San Jacinto on April 21, 1836, the *Yellowstone* was waiting nearby and received the wounded commander in chief, Sam Houston, the new Republic's interim president David G. Burnet, the captured Santa Anna and forty-seven Mexican prisoners.

Sam Houston said that had it not been for the service of the *Yellowstone*, the enemy would never have been overtaken. Houston related that "until they reached the Sabine use of the boat enabled me to cross the Brazos and save Texas."

Proudly, Captain John E. Ross and his crew had served Texas. They would do another great service by taking Austin's body to his family at Peach Point Plantation.

Austin's Grave

Austin was first buried at Gulf Prairie Cemetery in Brazoria County near Peach Point Plantation. In 1910, the body was reinterred at the Texas State Cemetery in Austin, Texas.

There are many statues of Stephen F. Austin. This one at the Texas State Cemetery with an inscription that says he was "wise, gentle, courageous and patient."

There are many other statues of Austin, including one that stands in the Capitol Building in Washington, DC, and at the Texas State Capitol in Austin, Texas. There is a huge statue of the Father of Texas at Angleton, Texas. He is well remembered by the great state of Texas.

# 6

## Dr. Robert Peebles's Life after San Felipe de Austin

*Honor a physician with the honor due unto him for the uses which ye may have of him; for the Lord hath created him.*

—(Apocrypha, Matthew 38:1)

Dr. Robert Peebles

During the time of the formation of the government in the new Republic of Texas, Dr. Peebles was involved in that new government. Just as his friend Stephen Austin had loved Texas and had a passion to see her grow, so did Dr. Peebles. Austin had chosen his friends in the Colony wisely.

## Dr. James Miller

Dr. Peebles had practiced medicine with Dr. James Miller in San Felipe, but now he was planning to move to another area of Texas. He had returned to his property on the Brazos in Fort Bend County after returning from New Orleans.

Both Drs. Miller and Peebles had been practicing physicians in San Felipe prior to Texas independence, and they had both been public officials. James Miller, a native of Kentucky, had represented the Fort Bend area in the Convention of 1833. He was one of the three commissioners designated to carry the petitions of that convention to Mexico. Instead, he remained in Texas to treat victims of a cholera epidemic. In 1834, he was a member of the legislature of Coahuila and Texas, which established the Department of the Brazos and made him its political chief. In that capacity, on July 2, 1835, he allocated $200 to maintain friendly relations with the northern Indians.

In 1835, he had pledged to offer armed resistance to the Mexican customs officials in Anahuac. Dr. Peebles, having been a close associate of Dr. Miller, knew of this and most likely supported his friend. By July 16, Miller wrote Domingo de Ugartechea, military commandant of Coahuila and Texas, about his role in the Anahuac Disturbances, assuring him that he had taken measures to "down the excitement."

He had written to the Mexican general again, protesting that the attack on Anahuac was not supported by a majority of the people and promising to dispatch a commission to San Antonio de Béxar to settle the misunderstanding.

About that time, Dr. Miller was informed that Gen. Martin Perfecto de Cos had issued arrest warrants for William B. Travis and Robert M. Williamson for their part in the disturbance. As a political chief, he was expected to issue warrants but was unwilling to have friends arrested for activities that he had himself encouraged.

Troubled by this state of affairs, he left San Felipe for his Fort Bend plantation. He sought the advice of friends as to what to do and one friend. Wyly Martin advised him to obey the law and issue the warrants. Dr. Miller could not bring himself to do so, and yet he could not refuse. On July 19, 1835, he turned in his resignation as political chief citing health reasons. He prevailed upon Martin to take his place while he took an extended leave to the hill country above Bastrop.

Dr. Peebles had been supportive of Dr. Miller's decision to step down rather than issue arrest warrants for friends with whom they totally agreed. He took care of their practice and attended to his own duties in the colony.

Upon his return, Dr. Miller became an active member of the Peace Party, which considered a declaration of independence premature. The organization did represent a faction of the Anglo-American population of Texas and tried to sway public opinion against armed conflict with the rest of Mexico in those crucial times from 1832 to 1835.

The counterpart of the Peace Party was, of course, the War Party. These were not political parties but just labels for persons opposing political dispositions. The Peace Party represented more Texans throughout that period and was critical of the War Party's agitation. Most Peace Party supporters joined the Texas Revolution. Stephen Austin had been a supporter of the Peace Party but was quick to join the Revolution when it seemed there was no other way than fight for independence.

When the battle of Gonzales ended any chance of reconciliation, Dr. Miller served under General Stephen Austin in October 1835. He aided in the organization of the Texas army, as did Dr. Peebles. They both supported, once adopted, the Texas Declaration of Independence. As partners in business, they were successful physicians, politicians, and landowners. Their service in Texas independence was invaluable.

Dr. Miller was a senator in the Fifth Congress of the Republic, 1840–1841. He was a secretary of the treasury under Sam Houston in 1843, as well as chief justice of Fort Bend County. He was a delegate to the Convention of 1845 but was defeated as candidate for governor in 1845 and 1847. In 1851, he was appointed one of the commissioners to investigate fraudulent land titles west of the Nueces River. Throughout his political career, he continued his medical practice and was well-known and highly respected as a physician. Although they didn't continue as partners, the doctors remained close friends throughout the remainder of their lives. Dr. Miller died in 1854 at the age of fifty-three.

In 1839, Dr. Peebles sold half of his grant to Dr. Miller. In 1840, the Austin tax roll listed Peebles as the holder of title to 1,062 acres of and worth $2,124 and an additional 1,800 acres under survey valued at $1,800.

## Dr. Peebles Establishes His Home in DeWitt County

On June 29, 1846, in DeWitt County, Dr. Peebles made bond to buy land from Joseph Kent. He may have sold that land or retained it, but the record shows that on May 1, 1849, he and his wife, Mary Trigg Peebles bought the Churchill Fulcher League of 4,428 acres for $4,000 cash in Dewitt County. They built a home on this land across the Guadalupe River from the town of Concrete. The home was about ten miles north of the town of Cuero with lands on both sides of the Guadalupe River.

Dr. and Mrs. Peebles were good Christian folks. On July 8, 1849, a group of settlers in the area gathered under a live oak tree at their home. That day, they formed the Live Oak Presbyterian Church, the first Presbyterian Church in DeWitt County. In 1855, the county's second Presbyterian Church was organized in Concrete. The churches later combined to form the Presbyterian Church of Cuero, Texas. A historic marker is on the spot of the live oak tree, and the church in Cuero that was first formed by the Peebles stands today.

Just as Dr. Peebles had been involved in the government during the time of the Austin Colony and the formation of the Republic, he served in 1842–43 representing Fort Bend County in the Seventh Congress of the Republic of Texas. In 1850, he was elected commissioner of DeWitt County. In November 1851, he was elected representative from DeWitt and Gonzales Counties to the Texas legislature. He gave up that position when he became ill and returned home, but there was yet plenty of work for him to do.

In 1853, Mary was to give birth to their first child. In July, she and the baby died. Obviously a devastating event, he returned her body to her family in New Orleans. Mary and her child were laid to rest in a family plot. In June 1854, he gave bond for $20,000 to administer her estate. The largest item in her estate was fifteen slaves. Her will names her only living brother,

Alanson Trigg, his minor children, and some nieces and nephews as heirs. Money from the sale of the slaves was divided between Dr. Peebles, the minor heirs of Alanson Trigg, Lucy Lane Kent, and Ellen Chenault.

In 1856, Peebles married Mary's niece Lucy Ann Trigg. She had been born in 1833 and was thirty-five years younger than Dr. Peebles. This may seem rather perverted by modern standards, but in those days, it was not uncommon to marry a cousin, even one that was much younger. Lucy, at least, was not a blood relative in this case. It was not uncommon for older widowed men to marry much younger women. To this union was born John O. McGhee Peebles, born January 21, 1859, and Katie E. Peebles, no date of birth.

The Civil War began, but there is no record on Dr. Peebles's sentiments on the war. By this time, he was sixty-two years of age. Sam Houston was opposed to secession, as were some of the others who had been supporters of annexation into the United

States. There was no fighting in the area of DeWitt County, so their lives went on as usual.

## Concrete College in Concrete Texas

In Concrete, Texas, soon after the Civil War, Dr. and Mrs. Lucy Peebles, along with other pioneer settlers in that area, sponsored and lobbied for the Concrete College. This was the first school in Concrete and was conducted by James Norman Smith, who had taught President James Polk in Tennessee. The college became a typical nineteenth-century rural college. By the mid-1870s, a ten-acre campus had taken shape along what was called Coon Hollow. The main building measured 150 by 50 feet, with a kitchen and dining room attached. Coeds shared the stone house of the Covey family, and the male students were assigned to more primitive, two-room frame buildings.

Rev. John Van Epps Covey had begun teaching in the community about 1864, and his curriculum for the college favored the classics and business. Music and penmanship were offered, and even farming techniques were taught in a cultivated area adjacent to the college. More than a dozen instructors taught an annual average of perhaps 100 students during the twenty-year existence of the college. Hebrew, Greek, and Latin fundamentals were covered, although these were languages of little use to the students upon graduating. Some pupils were admitted before the age of twelve and were taught some primary school subjects. The women teachers molded the social amenities in what was called the "ladies department." Sewing and musical talents were also on the curriculum, giving the students a well-balanced education, perhaps to the equivalency of more advanced high school education of today.

The college was Baptist-oriented, and the school's financial status was undertaken by the Texas Baptist Convention. In 1870, most of the boarders were males ranging in age from twelve to twenty. Most of them were Texans, although some were from Indiana and even as far away as Germany and England. The peak enrollment year of 1873–1874 had 250 students attending classes, and the 100 boarders came from twenty Texas counties. A fee of $100 covered tuition, room, and board for a five-month semester. For a time, the institution was the largest boarding school in the state.

The students' day at Concrete was well regulated, and the attire was carefully scrutinized. Firearms, profane language, alcohol, gambling, and smoking were all strictly forbidden. Graduation was a social event that lasted three days with concerts each evening.

Sadly, measles and influenza ravaged the student population in 1871 and 1872. In 1873, the Gulf, Western Texas, and Pacific Railway arrived in Cuero and shifted emphasis away from Concrete. The development of public schools within the county also contributed to the school's decline.

The Peebleses' son Johnny had not been old enough to attend the college in its heyday. He was sent back to Jackson, Tennessee, for his education, where his mother Lucy had relatives. For the time that the college was in the county, it made the difference in many lives. It was just one more noted accomplishment that Dr. Peebles did for Texas.

Today, near Cuero, Peebles descendants still live on the property. The Peebles Ranch is still run by descendants of the doctor who came to Austin's Colony and set out to make a difference.

Little has been known about Dr. Robert Peebles and his contributions to Texas. As an unsung hero, he did as much to save Texas, as did those at the Alamo or San Jacinto, if not more. Lest that be judged as a tall statement, we must not forget that he took the archives to a safe place. In that respect, he "saved Texas." Without those titles to lands, the documents, and other important letters, how could it be proven that the settlers owned their land?

Perhaps this is why Austin never reprimanded his friend Dr. Peebles in the same way he had Samuel Williams. The doctor had admitted his wrongdoing, returned that evidence, along with the other titles, and was absolved of any wrong doing.

Dr. Robert Peebles died of a stroke at his home July 12, 1871. He is buried on his property next to his beloved Mary Trigg Peebles and mother of his children, Lucy Trigg Peebles. Although he had owned vast properties, a good portion of the land was sold by his widow to pay taxes.

If he came to Texas today, he would be proud of this State, no doubt. He would love the monuments at Austin, Texas, the state cemetery and the magnificent Capitol building. To give him his place in history is an honor, and no one need confuse him with Dr. Richard Peebles and think that there was only one Dr. Peebles.

In my research of the two doctors, I found that even librarians at universities and museums thought the two doctors were one and that someone had just confused the names. It is time the record is set straight and their history written in a way that honors both men.

# 7

## Doctor Richard Rogers Peebles Finding His Place in History

> All these were honored in their generations, and were the glory of their times. There be of them that have left a name behind them, that their praises might be reported.
>
> —Apocrypha, Matthew

## Washington—Birthplace of the Republic

Dr. Richard Peebles and other residents of Washington were able to return to their homes after the defeat of the Mexican army. Washington had some ransacking but was mostly unscathed. After the Texas victory at San Jacinto, the rapid influx of new settlers into the interior and the expanding agricultural cultivation in Washington and surrounding areas augmented the town's significance as a supply and transit point. The proximity to the Brazos and location to other major roads gave this town where Texas independence began a bright future. This was the perfect place for the young doctor to continue his practice.

The town became the county seat, making it a legal center. Abundant timber in the vicinity encouraged sawmills, which began operating by 1837. A brickyard was established the same year, furthering more construction in the town. There was a Republic of Texas Post Office in the town, which gave area residents the convenience of mail service on a regular basis.

In 1837, Texans came from all sections of the Republic to attend a ball to celebrate the first anniversary of Texas independence. That was a day of sheer celebration after all that had happened in the past year. The dignitaries list was quite long, and the gaiety of the celebration was uplifting and joyous to all.

The town was incorporated by the Texas Congress on June 5, 1837, and reincorporated under a mayor-alderman form of city government on December 29, 1837. However, some of the townspeople went a little too far with the growth of the town after the incorporation. The construction of a race track, the proliferation of gambling and drinking establishments, and some rowdy, furloughed Texas army veterans resulted in a disorderly and lawless environment. It resulted in a halt in growth and some residents moving.

In 1837, Rev. Z. N. Morrell established the first Missionary Baptist Church at Washington. The Baptist, Methodist, and Cumberland Presbyterian clergyman united together to stop the lawlessness that was destroying the town. Never underestimate the power of a Christian movement. In 1840, a revival led by R.E.B Baylor and Rev. William Tryon generated a movement that ended most of the lawlessness. Washington became a center of religious activities and rid the town of its wicked ways—mostly.

The economic growth that ensued gave way to Washington becoming a center of education and journalism. In 1837, the first school was established bringing in more families with young children. By 1839, the town residents numbered 250, which is not much by today's standards but a thriving community for those days.

A depression in 1839 caused the commerce and population to wane, and Mount Vernon, another small but thriving town, became county seat in 1841. That year, Dr. Peebles had to make a decision about his practice. In 1841, he moved to Austin County, where he opened a general store and pharmacy.

He might have been a bit hasty on that decision as more progress and historical significance would descend upon Washington. In 1842, Washington became the capitol of Texas once again. During Sam Houston's second administration and the administration of his successor, Anson Jones, the Texas Congress, high courts, and foreign embassies moved in, and the town's economy and social life were stimulated. The town was also the site of peacemaking between President Houston and the Indians in the summer of 1844. Jones's inauguration and inaugural ball, as well as the session of the Texas Congress that approved annexation to the United States, occurred at Washington in 1845. When Austin became the capitol again in the late summer of 1845, the popular *Texas National Register* newspaper moved there as well. Washington lost its political significance but continued to have some significant growth.

The move to Austin County, which is not the same as Austin the Capitol, proved to be an important and rewarding move for Dr. Peebles. He rented a portion of the estate of the younger Jared E. Groce Jr. in 1842. This was not far from Washington and still a place where he did some business. Having his own store proved to be quite profitable for him at a time when his life at age thirty-three was changing dramatically. He had also received a grant for his services in the Revolution.

## The Groce Family of Bernado Plantation

Jared Ellison Groce Sr. was born in Virginia in 1782. His father had come to America from England and had been in George Washington's army. Groce had settled first in South Carolina at twenty years of age, investing in land that became quite valuable. In two years, he married Mary Ann Waller. The Waller family was a prominent one in both political and social life.

Soon after his marriage, he moved to Georgia and invested in a plantation. Four children were born to them there: Leonard Waller, Edwin, Sarah Ann, and Jared Ellison Jr. His wife died while visiting relatives in South Carolina in 1813 when her youngest child, Jared, was only one year old. After her death, the despair seemed to motivate Groce to move on to another location. He entered his children in college: Sarah Ann in Nashville, Tennessee, when she was only eleven years old and his boys in a college in Macon, Georgia. He sold his plantation and moved to Alabama, where he invested in thousands of acres in timberland, putting his slaves to work clearing them.

It was at this time the Mexican government offered great inducements to settlers to come Texas. For Jared Groce, this enticement would seemingly help his aching heart with adventure and excitement. He sold his land in Georgia and quickly made the move to Texas in January, 1822.

Groce built a plantation home on a high bluff on the Brazos River four miles south of the present site of Hempstead, which is now Waller County. He built a rambling story-and-a-half house of cottonwood logs, hewn, and counter hewn. When completed, it had four large rooms downstairs, two rooms, and a half upstairs, and a house-length gallery supported by polished walnut columns. The other plantation buildings included a kitchen, bachelor hall for entertaining guests, a dairy, and quarters for the house slaves. Near a small lake on the vast property were quarters for the field slaves, an overseer's house, a kitchen and dining hall, and a day nursery for children of the field workers. It included a doctor's house, which may have been the first doctor in Texas, but his name could not be found. It was an impressive place and perhaps the largest for that time in Austin's colony.

Cotton was planted, and Groce became the first large planter in Texas. He had plenty of slaves, over one hundred, and workers to harvest his crop and keep his plantation running in top-notch condition. In 1825, a gin was in operation on the property, and the whole production from start to finish was accomplished.

Groce's daughter, Sarah Ann, didn't return from school until she was seventeen. After graduation in New York, she came to Bernardo, accompanied by several relatives from South Carolina and Georgia. She would not be in the home for long as she had met William H. Wharton while attending school with his sister, Betsy, in Nashville. They were married December 5, 1827.

Within a few more years, both sons would be married. It was at this time that Groce decided to divide his property and slaves between his children. He had already given Sarah Ann her share of two leagues of land in Brazoria County and a large home called Eagle Island Plantation. Bernardo was given to his eldest son, Leonard.

Jared Jr. received a league next to Bernardo, on which he built his home Pleasant Hill. He married, on October 1, 1833, Mary Ann Calvit. They had two children: Jared Ellison III, born 1837, and Barbara Mackall, born 1838.

Edwin Groce was drowned in the Brazos River soon after he came to Texas. It seems that he was in a skiff with William Whorton and his sister, Sarah Ann, and their young son, John Austin. They were trying to cross the river while it was in a swollen condition, and the ferry was out of condition. It capsized when a large log floating down the river hit the ferry throwing them all into the water. Wharton succeeded in getting his wife and son to the bank, but when he returned for Edwin, he could not be found. Since Edwin was considered a good swimmer, it is thought that he must have been knocked unconscious by the log that overturned the skiff. The body was never found.

Groce Sr. was burdened with more than his share of grief. He felt he was too old and sick to continue running the plantation and had for a time moved to a smaller place, which was called The Retreat. Groce Sr. came back to Bernardo from March 31 to April 15, 1836, when the Texas army, under the command of General Sam Houston, camped near Groce's Ferry.

A hospital was set up for the soldiers; all plantation facilities were at the disposal of the general and his army. There were many refugees from the Runaway Scrape camping on the grounds or being sheltered and fed.

On April 12, the "Twin Sisters" were unloaded and placed in front of Bernardo. The two cannons had been donated to the cause by some citizens of Cincinnati, Ohio. Those cannons were the only "large" artillery used in the battle at San Jacinto. Sam Houston's army crossed the river on the *Yellowstone* steamboat on April 12–14.

Bernardo Plantation with the two cannons

Groce Sr. died November 20, 1836, and was buried at Bernardo. He had been one of the first to settle in Austin's Three Hundred Colony and became one of the most successful. Like Austin, he died soon after Texas became a republic. He, like Austin, had persuaded others to come to Texas. Upon realizing the abundant possibilities of the Texas soil and experiencing the delightful climate, he wrote back to the old States hundreds of letters, advising friends, relatives, and others to come to the "Land of Promise."

Austin was a great man and was rightly called the Father of Texas as he brought many colonists to Texas. However, Jared Groce Sr. was instrumental in bringing many, among them influential and prominent men who would help to make Texas great. He spared no money to advance the progress of his adopted country, but this was done in such a quiet and unobtrusive manner that no credit was ever given him. He is another relatively forgotten and unsung hero.

Leonard Waller Groce lived at Bernardo from 1833 to 1853, when he moved his family to a new home at Liendo Plantation, although he continued to own and plant at Bernardo until his death in 1873. Sadly, Bernardo was torn down in 1865 by William Wharton Groce in order to build a new home a few miles from Bernardo. The once famous plantation was fading into history.

Archaeologists have been combing through the site, which is fifty miles northwest of Houston. The project seeks to detail and preserve remains of Bernardo.

"If you read any of the early documents about the fight for Texas Independence, this plantation site figured prominently in that," said Jim Bruseth, director of the Texas Historical Archaeology division. "Anybody of any importance came through there."

Greg Brown, publisher of *Cowboys & Indians*, a magazine about the American West and owner of a Houston television station, purchased the 1,500-acre ranch several years ago.

"This is where plantation history began in Texas," said Light Cummins, the state historian, "This first major plantation and, in number of slaves, remains the largest plantation in the Republic of Texas. In terms of early history of Texas, this is where the South became the West."

# William H. Wharton

It seems there is a weaving of families that fit together in the whole story of Texas history. Wharton is one that plays a significant part in the whole tale.

Groce had, at one time, aroused the jealously of Austin, of whom it was known he desired to be chief and head of all, the reason being that Groce didn't go to Austin for advice as other settlers so often did. Groce didn't feel the need of Austin's care and protection. This was said to have incensed Austin. There was also a misunderstanding between Austin and Groce's son-in-law, William H. Wharton. Groce went about handling the situation in his quiet way by ignoring the situation. Reconciliation was brought about later between Austin and Wharton. Their personal feelings were put to rest because of their love for country, and they joined their efforts to defeat the enemy. It was believed by some that had this not taken place, Texas would not have won her freedom at that time. That would be doubtful in that several different factors were coming into play for Texas to gain Independence from Mexico.

It seems that Wharton wrote a personal letter to Sam Houston and was instrumental in persuading the future general and president to come to Texas. He had known Houston in Tennessee and was telling Jared Groce Sr. about Sam Houston and his success as a fighter. "That's the kind of men we need in Texas. Sit right down and write to him, urge him to come, and I will send the letter by the next post."

Wharton had served as a delegate to the Convention of 1832 and as a president of the follow-up Convention 1833 from the District of Victoria. He had openly advocated independence from Mexico, which was in contrast to the moderate held view by some native Texans and Stephen Austin. He later served as a delegate from the Columbia district to the Texas Consultation of 1835.

Wharton entered military service during the Texas Revolution, serving as a colonel and judge advocate general. He participated in the siege of San Antonio de Béxar. Shortly thereafter, he supported Austin's unsuccessful candidacy for president as they had become close friends. He went on to serve as a member of the new republic's Senate in the District of Brazoria in 1836.

In November 1836, President Houston appointed Wharton as a minister to the United States, hoping to secure political recognition and possible annexation. Returning by sea, he was captured by a Mexican ship and carried to Matamoros, where he was imprisoned. He escaped and returned to Texas to be reelected to the Texas Senate in 1838.

Wharton also has the distinction of having designed and introduced the Texas Lone Star flag to Congress. The knowledge of that accomplishment alone makes him quite the hero in Texas history.

On March 14, 1839, Wharton accidentally shot and killed himself while dismounting from his horse near Hempstead, Texas, in Waller County. Another Texas hero was laid to rest much too soon.

## Dr. Richard Peebles and the Groce Family

Dr. Peebles had been acquainted with almost every Texan written in Texas history who had helped to bring about Texas independence. He was there as a witness and participant in all the history that unfolded from the time he came to the colonies and thereafter. He, like so many others, would have made the trek to Columbia to pay last respects to Stephen F. Austin. He had not just been acquainted, but some were his personal and close friends. As a physician, he would have treated many of the colonists for a variety of ailments.

Jared Groce Jr.—or as some documents list him, Jared Groce II—died February 3, 1839. No record or document of the cause of death has been found. His young widow was left with two toddlers, a one-year-old and a two-year-old.

Dr. Peebles had known of, or even met, many in the Groce family when he inquired of leasing the deceased Jared Groce Sr.'s property. Setting up a pharmacy and general store would avail him to meet everyone in the community, including the widow, Mrs. Mary Ann Calvit Groce. Perhaps as a physician, he was called on when her children were ill.

There is probably a wonderful romance story in there, but it would have to be made up in that nothing has been recorded of their courtship. One can only imagine. A handsome young doctor and a lonely widow who met, become friends, and soon a courtship ensued.

After their marriage on March 8, 1843, he resided at his wife's plantation, Pleasant Hill. He became the stepfather to Mary Ann's five- and six-year-old children. He continued in his lucrative medical practice and businesses, which included caring for slaves in the area's many plantations.

Mary Ann kept a diary, which is in the Briscoe Center for American History in Austin. Part of the diary is a short detail of their life in 1854. They had nine children of their own, so theirs was a busy life. She always referred to her husband as Dr.

Peebles in her writings. It seems someone was always ill, including Mary Ann.

She wrote, "A beautiful day. I was quite sick last night and today. My husband was up with me most of the night. I feel better today."

She wrote of how often the children were ill and how the doctor took care of them and how they felt better quickly. This was one busy doctor, carrying for a large family and those in and around their community.

She also wrote of some trips to Ohio. They did have train transportation, which was a long trip, but much easier than going by a stage coach or wagon. They kept in close contact with the family in Ohio as she wrote in her diary.

## The Richest Man in Texas

In 1846, Dr. Peebles was elected an Austin County Justice of the Peace. His many entrepreneurial pursuits included a partnership in the brokerage and cotton-factoring firm of J. Shackelford and Company. He participated in the development of the Washington County Railroad and Houston and Central Texas Railway. By 1860, his railroad ventures and investments led him to become one of the wealthiest men in Texas. Some documents list him as being the richest man in Texas prior to the Civil War.

In 1856, Dr. Peebles founded the town of Hempstead, Texas, naming it for his brother-in-law Giles Samuel Booth Hempstead of Portsmouth, Ohio. He always maintained a close connection to his family in Ohio. Yet he could have named the town Peebles, as he had donated the land for the town.

In 1858, Washington, the town where once Dr. Peebles had called his first home in Texas, refused to pay the Houston and Texas Central Railroad the $11,000 bonus to link the town to the projected rail line. Construction of the Houston and Texas Central to Navasota in 1859 and of the Washington County

Railroad to Brenham in 1860 accelerated the rise of these towns and the decline of Washington, which had favored river transportation. With the increasing use of railroads, steamboats ceased to operate on the Brazos and the once-prosperous river port at Washington and other places along the river were doomed.

On February 20, 1860, Dr. Peebles presided at a public meeting at Bellville, Texas, to voice Southern grievances. He was a slaveholder, and his views of owning slaves may not have been his main concern. He did opposed succession. Many Texans opposed succession, including Sam Houston. Dr. Peebles made his concerns openly, which gave concern to those who were for Texas succeeding from the Union.

During the Civil War, he and four other Unionists were arrested for attempting to distribute a pamphlet advocating an end to the war. They were charged with treason by General John Bankhead McGruder on October 11, 1863. He and his companions appealed to the Texas Supreme Court for a writ of habeas Corpus, precipitating a jurisdictional dispute between Confederate military and civilian authorities. A civilian judge ordered them released on grounds of insufficient evidence, but General Kirby Smith ordered them to be arrested once again.

They were held in the Anderson jail, where the conditions were harsh, if not impossible. Dr. Peebles almost died of typhus, and during the imprisonment, he lost the sight in his left eye. In 1864, he and two other prisoners were deported to Mexico, but no reason for this deportation has been recorded.

Just prior to the end of the Civil War, he was in Monterrey, Matamoros. He didn't return to Hempstead, his family fearing he would be arrested, but rather traveled to New Orleans. From there, he did go to Portsmouth, Ohio, to visit relatives that he had not seen in years. He may have had Mary Ann and some of the children with him during that time.

Dr. Peebles returned to New Orleans in July 1865, where he was appointed a customs collector, most likely to earn enough money to return home. He would not have had access to his assets in Texas. He didn't return to Texas until August 1865.

He was in such poor health by the time he returned to Hempstead that he couldn't resume his medical practice. His stepson and son-in-law were managing his business affairs. An adverse court judgment in 1869 eventually resulted in the loss of what property he had not transferred to his children.

Dr. Peebles was an active Republican. This may have caused him some difficulty after the Civil War. He and Mary Ann donated land for a nominal fee to the Hempstead Freedman's School in 1870. Some Republicans tried unsuccessfully to name a proposed county for Peebles. It was instead designated as Waller County in 1873.

Dr. Richard Rogers Peebles, physician, entrepreneur, cotton farmer, railroad tycoon, and unsung hero would reach the age of eighty-three. From the wealthiest man in Texas to losing all his assets, he died August 8, 1893, at the home of his daughter, Gaylord, and was buried in Hempstead Cemetery.

It was not the end of the story or Dr. Peebles. At least one more thing would make him more famous than his wealth and his time in Texas history.

## The Ark of the Covenant of the Texas Declaration of Independence

R. Henderson Shuffler wrote,

> At eleven o'clock in the morning of February 27, 1961, President Harry H. Ransom of the University of Texas delivered to Governor Price Daniel one of the most interesting relics of the Republic of Texas, *The Ark of the Covenant of the Texas Declaration of Independence*. The ancient oblong wooden box is to occupy a place of honor in the new State Archives building on the Capitol grounds.
>
> In the custody of the University of Texas since 1927, the relic was this year brought out of storage and placed under the care of the Texas Library and Historical Commission. It is legally the property of the people of Texas.
>
> The battered old chest is the only physical relic of that strangely unknown building in which Texas' independence was declared on March 2, 1836, and in which the first Constitution of the Republic was adopted some fifteen days later. Built of hand split oak boards from the original building and veneered with walnut from the desk on which the Declaration was supposed to have been signed, the box is approximately fourteen inches wide, twenty-three inches long, and ten and a half inches deep. The inner lid bears handwritten inscription, and a small wooden tray is mounted in the upper right, just under the lid. Although the veneer is peeling in many places and some of the original fittings have been lost or damaged, the old chest is remarkably sound.

The box was made by John M. Gould, well-known cabinetmaker in the time of the Convention, and was presented by him to Dr. Richard Rogers Peebles, pioneer Texas physician. Dr. Peebles, like Gould, had been living in the town of Washington on March of 1836.

Exactly when this "Ark of the Covenant" was made, or when it was presented to Dr. Peebles, has not been determined. The fact that the authenticity of the source of the walnut veneer has been questioned indicates that Gould may have built the box years after the signing of the Declaration. Dr. Peebles's reference to himself in the inscription as being "of Austin County, Texas" indicates it was given to him after 1841 and perhaps much later.

Written on the wood inside the lid and still reasonably legible is this inscription:

> This box was made by Mr. John M. Gould, and by him presented to R.R. Peebles, of Austin County, Texas out of materials taken from a House in the Town of Washington, Texas, wherein sat the General Convention, which on the day of March, A.D. 1836, unanimously Resolved & Declared that the Political Relations heretofore Existing between the General Govm't of Mexico and her Texan Colony were, for just causes and substantial reason, from

that day & hour, considerately, formally and eternally ended, which Declaration of Independence, thus & then made a proclaimed, was gloriously verified & substantiated 'vi et armis,' on the Plain of San Jacinto, April 21, A.D. 1836. R. R. P.

The box was used by Dr. Peebles as a receptacle for letters and papers. As a man of considerable holdings and varied business interests, he no doubt had need for a receptacle. It was not, as some have thought, where the original Declaration of Texas Independence was kept, as it was in the possession of Dr. Peebles.

Upon Dr. Peebles's death in 1893, the relic passed to his daughter, Rachel. In 1927, this daughter, Mrs. Rachel Peebles White, and her husband, Reuben Grayden White of Hempstead, gave the box to the people of Texas. Their letter of donation:

To the People of Texas:
This box is made of wood taken from the first capitol of the Republic of Texas in which the Declaration of Independence was signed. This box contains facsimiles of the Declaration of Independence of Texas and memorial on education. It is our purpose to deliver this treasure to the people of Texas that they may keep it as did the people of Israel the "Ark of the Covenant" delivered to Moses.

R.G. White
R. P. White
Hempstead, Texas, Dec. 18, 1926

Late in 1926, the "Ark" was entrusted by Mr. and Mrs. White to the Reverend William Stuart Red of Austin, minister and historian, for presentation to the next Texas Independence Day. At Dr. Red's request, the formal presentation was made by his kinsman, Thomas S. Henderson of Cameron, noted attorney and orator. The presentation was made before a joint session of the House and Senate of the Texas Legislature, in the Capitol Building, on the evening of March 2, 1927. Representative Lee Satterwhite, former Speaker of the House of Representatives, presided at the meeting. After his introductory remarks, Sergeant Jack H. Drake blew a flourish on his bugle, calling attention to the procession entering the room. Three University of Texas coeds, members of the Orange Jackets, in uniform, bore the box, which was draped in a Texas flag. The procession was preceded by another Texas flag and was escorted by Lieutenant G. E. Shaw and Lieutenant W. Honacker.

This was quite a ceremony and presentation to honor Dr. Peebles and gave him his place in history. This "Ark" is housed today at the Briscoe Center for American History at the University of Texas at Austin.

## There Is a Reason for Peebles, Ohio

Although the town of Peebles, Ohio, has little to do with Dr. Richard Rogers Peebles, it is noteworthy and a bit of a side note to the Peebles connection. It is a town that recognized the contributions to the state of Ohio by the Peebles family.

The town is in a rural village in Adams County, Ohio. It was platted in 1881 and named in honor of John Geddes Peebles, brother of Dr. Richard Rogers Peebles. John Peebles, invested in the railroad business, was the man that persuaded the Cincinnati and Eastern Railway to run through the small town in order to create more business. As a result, the town became a booming place—at least for a time. At least one Peebles put his name on a town.

Surrounded by beautiful farmland in the Ohio River Valley, the area is graced by the Appalachian Mountains. The area today is home to many Amish families who appreciate the local rural heritage.

JOHN GEDDES PEEBLES.

It is this writer's belief that Dr. Richard Rogers Peebles was a humble man and was delighted that his brother, John, was honored. He may have even traveled to Ohio for the occasion of the dedication of the town.

The Peebles family left their mark on American and Texas history. Their story is an American success story.

# Epilogue

In researching for this book, I found many tidbits of information on the many individuals who had been a significant part of Texas Independence. For instance, Gail Borden Jr. had for the most part only been known as the founder of Borden's dairy products, especially condensed milk. From the historic records, it is interesting to see the roles others had to bring Texas to where it was and is truly like a "whole other country."

## Gail Borden Jr.'s Accomplishments

Borden resumed his business in publishing the Telegraph and Texas Register in Harrisburg in April 1836; in Columbia, 1836 to April 1837; and in Houston May and June of 1837. He also helped to lay out the site of Houston, where, for a time, Sam Houston as president of the republic located the capital. He sold his partnership in the Telegraph and became the first Customs Collector for the Department of the Brazos until 1837.

From 1839 to 1851, Borden was secretary and agent for the Galveston City Company, which owned most of Galveston Island. Perhaps the least of his accomplishments, but an important one, at least for some, was his invention of a "locomotive bath house" for women who wished to bathe in the Gulf of Mexico. As an alderman, he helped to temporarily rid the island of gamblers.

He and his wife, Penelope Mercer Borden, were reputedly the first Anglo-Americans to be baptized in the Gulf west of the Mississippi River. He was trustee of the Texas Baptist Education Society, which founded Baylor University.

In the mid-1840s, he began inventing, and it was supposed that he experimented with large-scale refrigeration as a means of preventing yellow fever. He developed a terraqueous machine (yes, that's right), a sort of prairie schooner that would go on land and water. In 1849, he perfected a meat biscuit (no, it was not McDonald's) made of dehydrated meat compounded with flour. The meat biscuit project left him deeply in debt as he struggled to sell meat biscuits. For this purpose, he moved to New York in 1851 to be nearer to the trade centers.

In 1853, he sought a patent on a process for condensing milk in a vacuum, but it was 1856 before he received American and British patents. Thankfully, he had enough sense to drop the meat biscuit and devote his time to condensing milk. He opened a factory in Connecticut but failed, then tried and failed again in 1857. He received backing from a New York financier and opened another factory in New York, one in Illinois, and licensed others in Pennsylvania and Maine. He also invented processes for condensing various fruit juices, extract for beef and coffee. The Civil War had brought intensified demand for condensed milk, and sales grew so much that success finally came to the Bordens in a big way. Finally, after the Civil War, he established a meat-packing plant at Borden, Texas (well, of course), twelve miles west of Columbus, bringing him back to his Texas roots. He established a sawmill and a copperware factory at Bastrop.

In the 1870s, he spent his winters in Texas to enjoy the milder climate. In 1873, he built a freedmen's school and a white children's school, organized a day school and a Sunday school for black children, aided in constructing five churches, maintained two missionaries, and partially supported numerous poorly paid teachers, ministers, and students.

He and his wife, Penelope, had seven children to carry on with the Borden name. Penelope had died in the 1840s, and he married Augusta Sterns. After her death, he married Emeline Eunice Church. No one can say that Gail Borden Jr. had not lived life to the fullest.

He died in Borden, Texas, on January 11, 1874; his body was shipped by private railroad car to New York to be buried in

Woodlawn Cemetery. The tombstone above his grave reads, "I tried and failed, I tried again and again and succeeded."

The addition of the story of Gail Borden Jr. to this book is only fitting in that he should be remembered for his many accomplishments. History should remember him not just for milk but for far more important accomplishments. It does seem strange, at least to me, that he is buried in New York and not in Texas at Austin in the Texas State Cemetery.

## Anson Jones—A President of the Republic

He was born in Massachusetts in 1878. He was licensed to practice medicine at the age of twenty-two. Immigrating to Texas in 1833, he settled in Brazoria. He was strongly in favor of Texas independence and did good work on the battlefield and in the hospitals.

He became a member of the Texas Congress, minister to the United States, and secretary of state before he became president. He was the last president of the Republic of Texas. At the annexation of Texas to the United States, he gave the following valedictory when he turned over the government to Governor J. Pickney Henderson:

> The great measure of annexation, so earnestly discussed, is happily consummated. The present occasion, so full of interest to us and all the people of this country, is an earnest of that consummation; and I am happy to greet you, their chosen representatives, and to tender to you my cordial congratulations on an event the most extraordinary in the annals of the world—one which makes a bright triumph in the history of republican institutions. A government is changed both in its officers and in its organization, not by violence and disorder, but by the deliberate and free consent of its citizens; and amid perfect and universal peace and tranquility the sovereignty of the nation is surrendered, and incorporated with that of another…The Lone Star of

> Texas, which ten years since arose amid clouds, over fields of carnage, and obscurely seen for a while, has culminated, and following an inscrutable destiny, has passed on and become fixed forever in that glorious constellation, which all freemen and lovers of freedom in the world must reverence and adore—the American Union. Blending its rays with its sister States, long may it continue to shine… The first act in the great drama is now performed. The Republic of Texas is no more.

President Jones retired to his plantation, where he busied himself with his professional and literary labors until 1858. For some reason, a depression overtook him, and he took his own life. His book, *Republic of Texas*, contains much valuable information for a student of Texas history.

## Thomas Jefferson Rusk

He was born in South Carolina in 1803. His education came from his friendship with John C. Calhoun, who had aided him in his pursuits. Rusk became licensed to practice law, moving first to Georgia. He visited Texas in 1834 and was determined to make Texas his home. Under President David G. Burnet, he became secretary of war.

He spent much time in the Texas camp during the fight for independence. In those darkest days, his eloquence roused the moral and drooping spirits of the patriot army. At the battle of San Jacinto, he was commended for his bravery. He was in the Texas Congress in 1837, but soon after that, he went to battle with the Indians, who were proving to be troublesome on the Texas frontier, and defeated them. After serving as chief justice, he was made president of the annexation convention and was elected United States Senator from Texas.

In 1856, the loss of his wife wrecked his health. To the surprise and grief of his friends, he committed suicide. In 1894, the state erected a monument over his grave in Nacogdoches.

## Guy M. Bryan

He was the son of Stephen F. Austin's sister, Emily Austin Bryan Perry, from her first marriage. He was born in Missouri in 1821 and came to Texas in 1831, along with his mother and stepfather, James Perry. During the Texas Revolution, in spite of his youth, he was entrusted as a courier to hear important news.

After graduating at Kenyon College, Ohio, he studied law, served in both houses of the legislature, and was elected to Congress. He entered the Civil War as a private to fight for the South and came out a colonel after having been sent on many missions by Confederate President Jefferson Davis and other Confederate leaders.

After the war, he returned to Congress and was Speaker of the fourteenth legislature. President Rutherford Hayes called him to the White House to confer with him concerning matter in the South. Colonel Bryan, with his allegiance to Texas, helped to organize the Texas Veterans' Association and the Daughters of the Republic.

At his death, which occurred in Austin in 1901, he gave as a priceless treasure to the University of Texas, the Austin Papers. These letters and documents left by his uncle, Stephen F. Austin, form the most valuable single collection in the Southwest.

## Many Unsung Heroes

There are so many other men and women of Texas history that will go unsung. In this account, I've tried to point out a few of those who were so vital to the Texas history story. The main purpose was to distinguish the Dr. Peebles, but their lives were so touched by the many heroes and bigger-than-life individuals that it became a quest to tell a bit of the story of some of the others.

Although Stephen F. Austin has the distinction of being the Father of Texas, his entire story may not always be told. His story is what gave the doctors their complete story. Without Stephen F. Austin, there would never have been a story. Without the "Makers of Texas," men like Sam Houston, Gail Borden Jr., those who gave their lives in the Alamo and Goliad, and the brave who dared to battle the Mexican dictator, there is no story.

It is my hope that some young Texan who has that same determination as those men who worked so hard to build Texas to what it is today will emerge. There have been many down through the decades who did so much for this great State. There are those leaders in Texas today who have shown their desire to keep Texas great.

God bless Texas!

# References

*An American Heritage Story—Tracing the Ancestry of William Henry Peoples and Elizabeth Washington Peoples.* Gloria Peoples-Elam, Tate Publishing and Enterprises, LLC, 2013.

*A History of Texas Revised – A History of Texas for Schools,* by Mrs. Anna J. Hardwicke Pennybacker, Published by Mrs. Percy V. Pennybacker, Austin, Texas, revised edition 1908.

*A History of Texas and Texans* by Frank W. Johnson. Ernest W. Winkler, Texas State Librarian, Eugene C. Baker, Ph.D, Professor of American History, The University of Texas. Published by American Historical Society, 1914.

Ancestry.com – tracing the histories of Peebles.

Peebles Family History by Elizabeth Alexander Muir Taylor, photo of Dr. Robert Peebles, Courtesy of Cuero Heritage Museum, Cuero, TX,

*Evolution of a State – Recollections of Old Texas Days* by Noah Smithwick, Gammel Book Company, 1900.

Briscoe Center for American History, The University of Texas Austin, Archival Papers of Dr. Richard Rogers Peebles and Dr. Robert Peebles. Robert U. Peebles Papers, 1832, 1834-1858, 1887. Deeds, correspondence, receipts and an account book. Correspondence (1835-1839) regarding the land records of Stephen F. Austin's colony and a list of land scripts. Plantation records from 1857 to 1860. A guide to Richard Rogers Peebles papers, 1840-1845, 1883.

Handbook of Texas Online, Information provided some histories of Austin's Three Hundred and Towns.

JSTOR online research --"Minutes of the Ayuntamiento at San Felipe de Austin" – 1829-1832; Recollections of Stephen F. Austin—George Hemmeken letter to Guy M. Bryan. "The Ark of the Covenant of the Texas Declaration" by R. Henderson Shuffler.

New International Version of the Holy Bible—Quotes at each chapter.

*Peebles Ante 1600 – 1960* by Anne Bradbury Peebles, Published by Anne Peebles, 1960. Genealogy of the Peebles/Peeples/Peoples families.

Portals of Texas, *Recollections of Stephen F. Austin, Austin Papers* – University of Texas at Austin; *Moses and Stephen F. Austin Papers*.

Prince George County Historical Society, Prince George, Virginia, Photos and Peebles History Courtesy of the Prince George County Archival Department.

Southwestern Historical Quarterly, Vol. 20, No 4 (April 1917), pp. 369-380, *Recollections of Stephen F. Austin—George Hammeken.* February 28, 1844.

Texas State Historical Association, "Land Speculation Cause of Texas Revolution" 1906, Page 80 thru 86. Histories of Dr. Robert Peebles, Dr. Richard Rogers Peebles, Dr. James Miller, William Wharton, Jared Groce and Family;

*Texas Yesterday and Today,* by L.W. Newton and Herbert P. Gambrell. Selected Readings From Texas History edited by Eugene C. Baker. Published by Turner Company, Dallas, Texas, 1949.

Washington-on-the-Brazos State Park, map and photos courtesy of the Texas State Park.

*With the Makers of Texas* –A Source Reader in Texas History, by Herbert Eugene Bolton, PH.D and Eugene C. Baker, M.A., Instructors in History at The University of Texas, Gammel-Statesman Publishing Co., Austin, Texas, 1904.

CPSIA information can be obtained
at www.ICGtesting.com
Printed in the USA
FSOW03n1406290916
25522FS